WRIGHT FAMILY LAND TAX RECORDS

1809-1850

NELSON COUNTY VIRGINIA

Robert N. Grant

HERITAGE BOOKS
2009

HERITAGE BOOKS
AN IMPRINT OF HERITAGE BOOKS, INC.

Books, CDs, and more—Worldwide

For our listing of thousands of titles see our website
at
www.HeritageBooks.com

Published 2009 by
HERITAGE BOOKS, INC.
Publishing Division
100 Railroad Ave. #104
Westminster, Maryland 21157

Copyright © 2009 Robert N. Grant

All rights reserved. No part of this book may be reproduced or transmitted in any form or by any means, electronic or mechanical, including photocopying, recording or by any information storage and retrieval system without written permission from the author, except for the inclusion of brief quotations in a review.

International Standard Book Numbers
Paperbound: 978-0-7884-4938-3
Clothbound: 978-0-7884-8160-4

WRIGHT FAMILY

LAND TAX LISTS

1809 TO 1850

NELSON COUNTY, VIRGINIA

Revised as of May 16, 2007

© 2008, Robert N. Grant
1394(051607)

Introduction To Appendix: Land Tax Records, Nelson County, Virginia

This document is an appendix to a larger work titled Sorting Some Of The Wrights Of Southern Virginia. The work is divided into parts for each family of Wrights that has been researched. Each part is divided into two sections; the first section is text discussing the family and the evidence supporting the relationships and the second section is a descendants chart summarizing the relationships and information known about each individual.

The appendices to the work (of which this document is one) present source records for persons named Wright by county and by type of record with the identification of the person named and their Wright ancestors to the extent known.

The source for the records listed in this appendix is the following:

    1)   Nelson County, Virginia, Land Tax Lists, available from the Virginia State Archives, 11th & Capitol Streets, Richmond, Virginia 23219.

The identification of a person or their ancestor by year and county indicates their year of death and county of residence at death. For example, "1763 Thomas Wright of Bedford County" indicates that this was the Thomas Wright who died in 1763 in Bedford County. If no state is listed after the county, the state is Virginia; counties in states other than Virginia will have a state listed after the county, as in "1876 William S. Wright of Highland County, Ohio".

A parenthetical after the name indicates an identification of the person when a place of death is not yet known, as in "John Wright (Goochland County Carpenter)". A county in parentheses after the name indicates the county with which that person was most identified when no evidence of the place of death has yet been found, as in "Grief Wright (Bedford County)".

All or portions of the text and descendants charts for each Wright family identified are available from the author:

    Robert N. Grant
    15 Campo Bello Court   (H) 650-854-0895
    Menlo Park, California 94025   (O) 650-614-3800

This is a work in process and I would be most interested in receiving additional information about any of the persons identified in these records in order to correct any errors or expand on the information given.

1809 LAND TAX LIST

NELSON COUNTY, VIRGINIA

Appendix: Nelson County, Virginia, 1809 Land Tax List:

A List of Land Taxed the County of Nelson 1809	Number of Acres __ Lot	Value p Acre	Whole Amount of Value	Tax	Identification
Moses Wright	100	.39	39.00	.19	1830 Moses Wright of Amherst County, son of 1799 Benjamin Wright of Amherst County and grandson of 1767 Francis Wright of Amherst County
	3	1.04	3.12	.02	
	71	.33	23.40	.11	
Archilles Wright	200	1.04	208.00	1.00	1825 Achilles Wright of Oldham County, Kentucky
	185	.26	48.10	.23	
Wm Wright	240	2.33	732.00	2.39	William Wright, Jr., son of William Wright (Amherst County)
Robt Wright	186	4.13	768.18	3.69	1816 Robert Wright of Nelson County, son of William Wright (Amherst County)
Andrew Wright	200	3.87	774.00	3.72	1816 Andrew Wright of Nelson County, son of William Wright (Amherst County)
James Wright	324	2.07	670.64	3.22	1839 James Wright of Nelson County, son of William Wright (Amherst County)
Jesse Wright	80	2.07	165.00	.81	1850 Jesse Wright of Nelson County, son of 1799 Benjamin Wright of Amherst County and grandson of 1767 Francis Wright of Amherst County
Estate Jordan Wright	138	1.04	143.52	.69	Estate of 1804 Jordan Wright of Amherst County, son of Parmenos Wright
John Wright (Son Robt)	199	1.04	206.96	.99	John Wright, son of 1816 Robert Wright of Nelson County and grandson of William Wright (Amherst County)

1810 LAND TAX LIST

NELSON COUNTY, VIRGINIA

Appendix: Nelson County, Virginia, 1810 Land Tax List:

A List of Land Tax the County of Nelson 1810	Number of Acres	Value p Acre	Whole Amount of Value	Tax	Identification
Moses Wright	100	.39	39.00	.19	1830 Moses Wright of Amherst County, son of 1799 Benjamin Wright of Amherst County and grandson of 1767 Francis Wright of Amherst County
	3	1.04	3.12	.02	
	71	.33	23.43	.11	
Archilles Wright	200	1.04	208.00	1.00	1825 Achilles Wright of Oldham County, Kentucky
	185	.26	48.10	.23	
Wm Wright	240	2.33	732.00	2.39	William Wright, Jr., son of William Wright (Amherst County)
Robt Wright	186	4.13	768.18	3.69	1816 Robert Wright of Nelson County, son of William Wright (Amherst County)
Andrew Wright	200	3.87	774.00	3.72	1816 Andrew Wright of Nelson County, son of William Wright (Amherst County)
John Wright (BS) House & Lot			40.00	.63	John Wright, son of 1839 James Wright of Nelson County and grandson of William Wright (Amherst County)
James Wright	324	2.07	670.64	3.22	1839 James Wright of Nelson County, son of William Wright (Amherst County)
	99	.33	32.67	.16	
Jesse Wright	80	2.07	165.00	.81	1850 Jesse Wright of Nelson County, son of 1799 Benjamin Wright of Amherst County and grandson of 1767 Francis Wright of Amherst County
Estate Jordan Wright	138	1.04	143.52	.69	Estate of 1804 Jordan Wright of Amherst County, son of Parmenos Wright
John Wright (Son Robt)	199	1.04	206.96	.99	John Wright, son of 1816 Robert Wright of Nelson County, and grandson of William Wright (Amherst County)

1811 LAND TAX LIST

NELSON COUNTY, VIRGINIA

Appendix: Nelson County, Virginia, 1811 Land Tax List:

A List of Land tax in Nelson County 1811	Number of Acres each lot contains	Value p Acre	Whole Amount of Value	Tax	Identification
Moses Wright	100	.39	39.00	.19	1830 Moses Wright of Amherst County, son of 1799 Benjamin Wright of Amherst County and grandson of 1767 Francis Wright of Amherst County
	3	1.04	3.12	.02	
	71	.33	23.43	.11	
Wm Wright	240	2.33	732.00	2.39	William Wright, Jr., son of William Wright (Amherst County)
Robert Wright	186	4.13	768.18	3.69	1816 Robert Wright of Nelson County, son of William Wright (Amherst County)
Andrew Wright	200	3.87	774.00	3.72	1816 Andrew Wright of Nelson County, son of William Wright (Amherst County)
John Wright (BS) House & Lot			40.00	.62	John Wright, son of 1839 James Wright of Nelson County and grandson of William Wright (Amherst County)
James Wright	324	2.07	670.64	3.22	1839 James Wright of Nelson County, son of William Wright (Amherst County)
	99	.33	32.67	.16	
Jesse Wright	80	2.07	165.00	.81	1850 Jesse Wright of Nelson County, son of 1799 Benjamin Wright of Amherst County and grandson of 1767 Francis Wright of Amherst County
	50	.16	8.00	.04	
Estate Jordan Wright	138	1.04	143.52	.69	Estate of 1804 Jordan Wright of Amherst County, son of Parmenos Wright
John Wright (Son Robt)	199	1.04	206.96	—	John Wright, son of 1816 Robert Wright of Nelson County, and grandson of William Wright (Amherst County)

1394(051607)

1812 LAND TAX LIST

NELSON COUNTY, VIRGINIA

Appendix: Nelson County, Virginia, 1812 Land Tax List:

A List of Land Tax in the County of Nelson 28th February 1812 Persons Names	Number of Acres	Value p Acre	Whole Amount of Valuation	Tax	Situation of each tract of Land & its boundaries	Identification
John Wright (BS) House & Lot			40.00	.63	Lys in Lovingston No 3	John Wright, son of 1839 James Wright of Nelson County and grandson of William Wright (Amherst County)
Robert Wright	187	4.13	768.18	3.69	on the Waters & Rkfish adj Jno Melton	1816 Robert Wright of Nelson County, son of William Wright (Amherst County)
Andrew Wright	200	3.87	774.00	3.72	on the Waters Rkfish adj Jos Shelton(?)	1816 Andrew Wright of Nelson County, son of William Wright (Amherst County)
John Wright (Son Robt)	363	1.04	377.52	1.80	On the Water Dutch Creek adj Theo Glass	John Wright, son of 1816 Robert Wright of Nelson County and grandson of William Wright (Amherst County)
James Wright	324	2.07	670.64	3.22	On the Water Daves Creek adj Lee W Hariss	1839 James Wright of Nelson County, son of William Wright (Amherst County)
	99	.33	32.67	.16	adj the above 324 Acres	
William Wright (attorney)	166	2.33	389.78	1.88	on Waters Daves creek adj Nathan ____	William Wright, Jr., son of William Wright (Amherst County)
Jesse Wright	80	2.07	165.00	.81	on Piny River adj John Camden	1850 Jesse Wright of Nelson County, son of 1799 Benjamin Wright of Amherst County and grandson of 1767 Francis Wright of Amherst County
	50	.16	8.00	.04	on Jas Do adj D S Garland	
Moses Wright	100	.39	39.00	.19		1830 Moses Wright of Amherst County, son of 1799 Benjamin Wright of Amherst County and grandson of 1767 Francis Wright of Amherst County
	3	1.04	3.12	.02		
	71	.33	23.43	.11		
Estate Jordan Wright	138	1.04	143.52	.69	Lys on Tye River adjs Saml Edmond	Estate of 1804 Jordan Wright of Amherst County, son of Parmenos Wright

1813 LAND TAX LIST

NELSON COUNTY, VIRGINIA

Appendix: Nelson County, Virginia, 1813 Land Tax List:

A List of Land Tax in the County of Nelson 28 Feby 1813	number of acres	Value p acre	Whole amt of Value	Tax	Situation of each tract of Land & its boundaries	Identification
John Wright (BS) house & lot			$75.00	1.56	In Lovingston No 3	John Wright, son of 1839 James Wright of Nelson County and grandson of William Wright (Amherst County)
Ro Wright	—	4.15	768.15	4.92	on waters rockfish adj adj Jno Melton &c	1816 Robert Wright of Nelson County, son of William Wright (Amherst County)
Andrew Wright	200	3.87	774.00	4.96	on waters rockfish adj Jos Shelton &c	1816 Andrew Wright of Nelson County, son of William Wright (Amherst County)
John Wright (SR)	363	1.04	377.52	2.40	on waters dutch creek adj T Glass &c	John Wright, son of 1816 Robert Wright of Nelson County, and grandson of William Wright (Amherst County)
Jas. Wright	324	2.07	670.64	4.29)	On Waters Davis creek adj	1839 James Wright of Nelson County, son of William Wright (Amherst County)
	99	.33	32.67	.21)	L W Harris &c	
Wm Wright	166	2.33	389.78	2.50	on waters Davis creek adjg A. Wright	William Wright, Jr., son of William Wright (Amherst County)
Jesse Wright	80	2.07	165.00	1.08	on Piney river adjg Jno Camden &c	1850 Jesse Wright of Nelson County, son of 1799 Benjamin Wright of Amherst County and grandson of 1767 Francis Wright of Amherst County
	50	.16	8.00	.05	on waters do adj D S Garland &c	
Moses Wright	100	.39	39.00	.25		1830 Moses Wright of Amherst County, son of 1799 Benjamin Wright of Amherst County and grandson of 1767 Francis Wright of Amherst County
	3	1.04	3.12	.03		
	71	.35	23.42	.14		
Estate Jordan Wright	138	1.04	143.50	.82	on Tye river adj S. Edmonds &c	Estate of 1804 Jordan Wright of Amherst County, son of Parmenos Wright

1814 LAND TAX LIST

NELSON COUNTY, VIRGINIA

Appendix: Nelson County, Virginia, 1814 Land Tax List:

	Residence	Estate	No. Town Lotts	Name of Town	Yearly rent of Lotts	Amount taxes on lotts at rate of ___	No of Acres of Land	Description of Land	Distance & bearing from the Courthouse	Rate of __ per acre	Total amount of __ of Land
John Wright BS	Nelson	Fee	No	Lovingston	$75	207					
Ro. Wright	Nelson	Fee					181	on waters rock Crk aj John Milton &	North 1 mile	4.13	768.15
Andrew Wright	Nelson	Fee					200	on waters rock Crk adj J Shelton &	North 6 miles	3.87	774.00
John Wright (Son Ro)	Nelson	Fee					363	on waters dutch aj _ T Glass &	East 11 miles	1.04	377.52
James Wright	Nelson	Fee					324)	on Davis creek	North 3 miles	2.07	670.61
	do	do					99)	W H Hutton &		.33	32.67
Wm Wright	Nelson	Fee					166	on Davis creek aj A Wright &	North 4 miles	2.33	389.78
Jesse Wright	Nelson	Fee					80	on Piny river ad Jno _der &	West 17 miels	2.67	165.00
							50	on Waters do ad D S Garland &		.16	8.00
Moses Wright							100			.39	39.00
							3			1.04	3.12
							71			.33	23.42
Estate Jordan Wright							138	on Tye river adj _ Edmunds &	South 9 miles	1.04	143.52

1394(051607)

12.

Appendix: Nelson County, Virginia, 1814 Land Tax List:

[continued from prior page]	Amount land at	Total Tax on Lotts & Land	Explanation of the preceeding Year	Identification
John Wright BS		2.07		John Wright, son of 1839 James Wright of Nelson County and grandson of William Wright (Amherst County)
Ro. Wright	6.56	6.56		1816 Robert Wright of Nelson County, son of William Wright (Amherst County)
Andrew Wright	6.61	6.61		1816 Andrew Wright of Nelson County, son of William Wright (Amherst County)
John Wright (Son Ro)	3.21	3.21		John Wright, son of 1816 Robert Wright of Nelson County, and grandson of William Wright (Amherst County)
James Wright	5.72 .27	5.99		1839 James Wright of Nelson County, son of William Wright (Amherst County)
Wm Wright	3.33	3.33		William Wright, Jr., son of William Wright (Amherst County)
Jesse Wright	1.43 .06	1.49		1850 Jesse Wright of Nelson County, son of 1799 Benjamin Wright of Amherst County and grandson of 1767 Francis Wright of Amherst County
Moses Wright	.33 .03 .18	.54		1830 Moses Wright of Amherst County, son of 1799 Benjamin Wright of Amherst County and grandson of 1767 Francis Wright of Amherst County
Estate Jordan Wright	1.09	1.09		Estate of 1804 Jordan Wright of Amherst County, son of Parmenos Wright

1815 LAND TAX LIST

NELSON COUNTY, VIRGINIA

Appendix: Nelson County, Virginia, 1815 Land Tax List:

Name of Owners	Residence	Estate	No. Town Lots	Name of Town	yearly rent	amt Tax on __ at rate of __	Number of acres of Land	Description of Land	Distance and bearing from __ House	Rate of Land pr acre	Total amount on __
John Wright BS		Fee	No	Lovingston	75	2.77	8½	on waters ruckers run adj N. Loftus &	West ¼ do	1.04	8.84
James Wright	do	Fee					324)	on Davis creek adj W H Shelton	North 3 do	2.07	670.64
	do	do					99)			.33	32.67
Robert Wright	Nelson	Fee					181	on waters rockfish aj John Melton &	South 1 do	4.13	768.15
Andrew Wright	Nelson	Fee					200	on waters rockfish adj Joseph Shelton &c	South 4 do	3.87	774.00
Jno Wright (SR)	Nelson	Fee					363	on waters dutch creek aj __ Thos Glass &	N of E 4 do	1.04	377.52
Wm Wright	Nelson	Fee					166	on Davis creek aj A Wright &c	North 4 do	2.33	389.78
Jesse Wright	Nelson	Fee					80	on Piny river aj Jno Camden &c	West 17 do	2.07	165.00
							50			.16	8.00
Moses Wright	Do	—					100			.39	39.00
							3			1.04	5.12
							71			.33	25.42

1394(051607)

Appendix: Nelson County, Virginia, 1815 Land Tax List:

Name of owners [continued from prior page]	Total tax on land by ____ ____	Total ____ ____	explanation of _____ the preceeding Year	Identification
John Wright BS	.06	2.83	____	John Wright, son of 1839 James Wright of Nelson County and grandson of William Wright (Amherst County)
James Wright	3.72 .27	5.99		1839 James Wright of Nelson County, son of William Wright (Amherst County)
Robert Wright	6.61	6.61		1816 Robert Wright of Nelson County, son of William Wright (Amherst County)
Andrew Wright	6.61	6.61		1816 Andrew Wright of Nelson County, son of William Wright (Amherst County)
Jno Wright (SR)	3.21	3.21		John Wright, son of 1816 Robert Wright of Nelson County, and grandson of William Wright (Amherst County)
Wm Wright	3.33	3.33		William Wright, Jr., son of William Wright (Amherst County)
Jesse Wright	1.43 .06	1.49		1850 Jesse Wright of Nelson County, son of 1799 Benjamin Wright of Amherst County and grandson of 1767 Francis Wright of Amherst County
Moses Wright	.33 .03 .18	.54		1830 Moses Wright of Amherst County, son of 1799 Benjamin Wright of Amherst County and grandson of 1767 Francis Wright of Amherst County

Appendix: Nelson County, Virginia, 1815 Land Tax List:

Name of Owners	Residence	Estate	No. Town Lots	Name of Town	yearly rent	amt Tax on __ at rate of __	Number of acres of Land	Description of Land	Distance and bearing from __ House	Rate of Land pr acre	Total amount on __
Est. Jordan Wright							138	on Tye river aj S Edmunds	South 9 do	1.04	143.52
Wm Wright	do	do					100	adj Parmenas Bryant &c	South 6 do	2.00	200.00

Appendix: Nelson County, Virginia, 1815 Land Tax List:

Name of owners [continued from prior page]	Total tax on land by ____ ____	Total ____ ____	explanation of _____ the preceeding Year	Identification
Est. Jordan Wright	1.09	1.09		Estate of 1804 Jordan Wright of Amherst County, son of Parmenos Wright
Wm Wright	1.70	1.70	from W Lilliput(?)	1851 William Wright of Amherst County, probably son of William Wright, Jr., and grandson of William Wright (Amherst County)

1816 LAND TAX LIST

NELSON COUNTY, VIRGINIA

Appendix: Nelson County, Virginia, 1816 Land Tax List:

Name of Owners	Residence	Estate	No of Town Lots	Name of Town	Yearly rent on Value	Amt of Tax on on Lots	Number acres of Land	Description of Land	Distance & Bearing from the Ct. House	Rate of Land pr acre	Total amt of Value of Land
Jno Wright BS	do	Fee	No	_	75	2.75	8½	on waters _ _ J Loving &c	West ½ do	1.04	8.84
James Wright	do	Fee					324) 99)	on Davis creek aj W H Shelton	N 3 do	2.07 .33	670.64 32.67
Robert Wright	do	Fee					181	on waters rock-fish aj Jno Melton &	N 1 do	4.13	768.15
Andrew Wright	do	Fee					200) 88) 72) 51)	on waters rock-fish adj W. Wright &c	N 4 do	3.87 .78 .84 .67	774.00 68.64 60.48 54.17
Wm Wright	do	Fee					166	on waters rock-fish adj A Wright &c	N 4 do	2.33	389.98
Jesse Wright	do	Fee					80) 50)	on Piny river aj Jno Camden &c	W 17 do	2.07 .16	165.00 8.00
Moses Wright							100 3 71			.39 1.04 .33	39.00 5.12 25.42
Est Jordan Wright							138	on Tye river aj S Edmunds &	S 9 do	1.04	143.52

Appendix: Nelson County, Virginia, 1816 Land Tax List:

Name of Owners [continued from prior page]	Total Tax upon Land	Total Tax upon Lots & Land	Explanation of all alterations During the preceding Year	Identification
Jno Wright BS	.06	2.51		John Wright, son of 1839 James Wright of Nelson County and grandson of William Wright (Amherst County)
James Wright	5.03 .25	5.28		1839 James Wright of Nelson County, son of William Wright (Amherst County)
Robert Wright	5.76	5.76		1816 Robert Wright of Nelson County, son of William Wright (Amherst County)
Andrew Wright	5.81 .53 .45 .26	7.05	from Est Peter Martin	1816 Andrew Wright of Nelson County, son of William Wright (Amherst County)
Wm Wright	2.92	2.92		William Wright, Jr., son of William Wright (Amherst County)
Jesse Wright	1.24 .52	1.30		1850 Jesse Wright of Nelson County, son of 1799 Benjamin Wright of Amherst County and grandson of 1767 Francis Wright of Amherst County
Moses Wright	.30 .03 .19	.52		1830 Moses Wright of Amherst County, son of 1799 Benjamin Wright of Amherst County and grandson of 1767 Francis Wright of Amherst County
Est. Jordan Wright	1.08	1.08		Estate of 1804 Jordan Wright of Amherst County, son of Parmenos Wright

1394(051607)

Appendix: Nelson County, Virginia, 1816 Land Tax List:

Name of Owners	Residence	Estate	No of Town Lots	Name of Town	Yearly rent on Value	Amt of Tax on on Lots	Number acres of Land	Description of Land	Distance & Bearing from the Ct. House	Rate of Land pr acre	Total amt of Value of Land
Wm Wright	do	do					100	on waters Tye river aj P. Bryant &	S 6 do	2.00	200.00

Appendix: Nelson County, Virginia, 1816 Land Tax List:

Name of Owners [continued from prior page]	Total Tax upon Land	Total Tax upon Lots & Land	Explanation of all alterations During the preceding Year	Identification
Wm Wright	1.50	1.50		1851 William Wright of Amherst County, probably son of William Wright, Jr., and grandson of William Wright (Amherst County)

1817 LAND TAX LIST

NELSON COUNTY, VIRGINIA

Appendix: Nelson County, Virginia, 1817 Land Tax List:

District of Benjamin Mosby:

Names of the Owners of Lands	Residence	Estate	No of Town Lots	Names of Town	Yearly rent or value	Amount of Tax on Lots at rate of	Number of Acres of Lands	Description of Land	Distance and bearing from the Court House	Rate of Land pr Acre	Total amount of the value of land
John Wright (B.S.)	Nelson	Fee		Lovgston	$75	$2.25	8½	on waters Ruckers River adj J Loving &c	W. 74 do	1.08	8.84
James Wright	Nelson do	Fee do					324) 98)	on Davis Crek aj W H Shelton &c	N 3 do	2.07 .33	670.64 32.67
Jno Wright (S to R)	Nelson	Fee					181	on waters Rockfish adj J Meltons	N 1 do	4.13	786.15
Est. Andrew Wright							200) 88) 72) 51)	on waters Rockfish adj Wm Wright	N 4 do	3.87 .78 .84 .67	774.00 68.64 60.48 34.17
Wm Wright	Nelson	Fee					166	on same adj A Wright &c	N 4 do	2.33	389.98
Jesse Wright	Nelson	Fee					80) 50)	on Piny River adj J. Camden &c	W 17 do	2.07 .16	165.00 8.00
Moses Wright	Nelson	Fee					100 3 71			.39 1.04 .33	39.00 3.12 23.42

1394(051607)

Appendix: Nelson County, Virginia, 1817 Land Tax List:

District of Benjamin Mosby:

Names of the Owners of Lands [continued from prior page]	Total Taxes upon Land	Total Tax upon Lots and Lands	Explanation of all Alterations during the preceding Year	Identification
John Wright (B.S.)	.06	2.31		John Wright, son of 1839 James Wright of Nelson County and grandson of William Wright (Amherst County)
James Wright	5.03 .25	5.28		1839 James Wright of Nelson County, son of William Wright (Amherst County)
Jno Wright (S to R)	5.76	5.76	from Est Ro. Wright decd.	John Wright, son of 1816 Robert Wright of Nelson County and grandson of William Wright (Amherst County)
Est. Andrew Wright	5.81 .53 .45 .26	7.05		Estate of 1816 Andrew Wright of Nelson County, son of William Wright (Amherst County)
Wm Wright	2.92	2.92		William Wright, Jr., son of William Wright (Amherst County)
Jesse Wright	1.24 .06	1.30		1850 Jesse Wright of Nelson County, son of 1799 Benjamin Wright of Amherst County and grandson of 1767 Francis Wright of Amherst County
Moses Wright	.30 .03 .19	.52		1830 Moses Wright of Amherst County, son of 1799 Benjamin Wright of Amherst County and grandson of 1767 Francis Wright of Amherst County

Appendix: Nelson County, Virginia, 1817 Land Tax List:

District of Benjamin Mosby:

Names of the Owners of Lands	Residence	Estate	No of Town Lots	Names of Town	Yearly rent or value	Amount of Tax on Lots at rate of	Number of Acres of Lands	Description of Land	Distance and bearing from the Court House	Rate of Land pr Acre	Total amount of the value of land
Est Jordan Wright							138	on Tye River aj S Edmunds &c	S 9 do	1.00	143.52
William Wright	Nelson	Fee					100	on Tye Rriver adj P. Bryant &	S 6 do	2.00	200.00
Benjn Wright							81	on head branches of South branch of Tye River		.20	16.20
Benjamin Wright							103	do do do		.20	20.60

Appendix: Nelson County, Virginia, 1817 Land Tax List:

District of Benjamin Mosby:

Names of the Owners of Lands [continued from prior page]	Total Taxes upon Land	Total Tax upon Lots and Lands	Explanation of all Alterations during the preceding Year	Identification
Est. Jordan Wright	1.08	1.08		Estate of 1804 Jordan Wright of Amherst County, son of Parmenos Wright
William Wright	1.50	1.50		1851 William Wright of Amherst County, probably son of William Wright, Jr., and grandson of William Wright (Amherst County)
Benjn Wright	.15	.15	New Grant	
Benjamin Wright	.21	.21	New Grant	

1818 LAND TAX LIST

NELSON COUNTY, VIRGINIA

Appendix: Nelson County, Virginia, 1818 Land Tax List:

Names of Persons	Residence	Estate	No of Town Lotts	Names of Town	Yearly Rent or Value	Amount of Tax on Lotts	Number Acres of Land	Description of Land	Distance & Bearing from the Ct. House	Rate of Land pr Acre	Total Amount Value of Land
John Wright (BS)	Nelson	Fee	No No	Lovg do	50$ 40	2.40 1.20	8½	adj Lovingston	W. ¼ do	1.04	8.84
James Wright	Nelson do	Fee do					324) 98)	on Davis Creek adj H. Shelton &c	N 3 do .33	2.07 32.67	670.64
Jno Wright (S to R)	Nelson	Fee					181	on waters rock-fish adj Jno Shelton's &	N 1 do	4.13	768.15
Est. Andrew Wright	Nelson	Fee					200) 88) 72) 51)	on waters rock-fish adj W Wright &c	do 4 do	3.87 .78 .84 .67	774.00 68.64 60.48 34.17
William Wright	Nelson	Fee					166	on waters rock-fish adj Est Andrew Wright &c	N 4 do	2.33	389.98
Jesse Wright	Nelson	Fee					80) 50)	on Tye river adj John Camden &c	W 17 do .16	2.07 8.00	165.00
Moses Wright	Nelson	Fee					100) 3) 71)			.39 1.04 .33	39.00 3.12 23.42

Appendix: Nelson County, Virginia, 1818 Land Tax List:

Names of Persons [continued from prior page]	Total Tax on Land	Total Tax on Lotts and Land	Explanations of all alterations During the Preceeding Year	Identification
John Wright (BS)	.06	3.66		John Wright, son of 1839 James Wright of Nelson County and grandson of William Wright (Amherst County)
James Wright	5.03 .25	5.28		1839 James Wright of Nelson County, son of William Wright (Amherst County)
Jno Wright (S to R)	5.76			John Wright, son of 1816 Robert Wright of Nelson County and grandson of William Wright (Amherst County)
Est. Andrew Wright	5.81 .53 .45 .20	7.05		Estate of 1816 Andrew Wright of Nelson County, son of William Wright (Amherst County)
William Wright	2.92	2.92		William Wright, Jr., son of William Wright (Amherst County)
Jesse Wright	1.24 .06	1.30		1850 Jesse Wright of Nelson County, son of 1799 Benjamin Wright of Amherst County and grandson of 1767 Francis Wright of Amherst County
Moses Wright	.30 .03 .19	.52		1830 Moses Wright of Amherst County, son of 1799 Benjamin Wright of Amherst County and grandson of 1767 Francis Wright of Amherst County

1394(051607)

Appendix: Nelson County, Virginia, 1818 Land Tax List:

Names of Persons	Residence	Estate	No of Town Lotts	Names of Town	Yearly Rent or Value	Amount of Tax on Lotts	Number Acres of Land	Description of Land	Distance & Bearing from the Ct. House	Rate of Land pr Acre	Total Amount Value of Land
Est Jordan Wright	Nelson	Fee					138	on Tye river adj Saul Edmunds &c	S 9 do	1.04	143.52

Appendix: Nelson County, Virginia, 1818 Land Tax List:

Names of Persons [continued from prior page]	Total Tax on Land	Total Tax on Lotts and Land	Explanations of all alterations During the Preceeding Year	Identification
Est Jordan Wright	1.08	1.08		Estate of 1804 Jordan Wright of Amherst County, son of Parmenos Wright

1819 LAND TAX LIST

NELSON COUNTY, VIRGINIA

Appendix: Nelson County, Virginia, 1819 Land Tax List:

Names of Owners	Residence of Owner	Estate	Number of Town Lots	Name of Town	Yearly rent or Value	Amount of Tax on Lots	Number Acres of Land	Description of Land	Distance and bearing from the Court House	Rate of Land pr Acre	Total Amount of Value of Land
John Wright	Nelson	fee	No	Lovingston	$80	$2.40	8½	adjoining Lovingston	N 400 yards	1.06	8.84
same	"	"	No	"	$40	$1.20					
James Wright	Nelson	fee					324	on the waters of Davis' Creek adj Wm H Shelton	N 3 M	2.07	670.68
same	"	"					98			.33	32.34
Estate of Andrew Wright	Nelson	fee					200	on the waters of Davis Creek adj Jos Shelton	N 4 M	3.87	774.00
same	"	"					88		" " "	.78	68.64
same	"	"					72		" " "	.84	60.48
same	"	"					51		" " "	.67	34.17
William Wright	Nelson	fee					166	on the waters of The Estate of Andrew Wright	N 4 M	2.33	386.78
Jesse Wright	Nelson	fee					80	on Piney River adj John Camden	W 17 M	2.07	165.60
same							50		.16	8.00	
Moses Wright	Amherst	fee					100			.39	39.00
same	"	"					3			1.04	3.12
same	"	"					71			.33	23.42

Appendix: Nelson County, Virginia, 1819 Land Tax List:

Names of Owners [continued from prior page]	Total Tax on Land	Total Tax on lots and Land	Explanation of all alterations during the preceeding year	Identification
John Wright	.06	2.46		John Wright, son of 1839 James Wright of Nelson County and grandson of William Wright (Amherst County)
same		1.20		
James Wright	5.03			1839 James Wright of Nelson County, son of William Wright (Amherst County)
same	.25	5.28		
Est. Andrew Wright	5.81			Estate of 1816 Andrew Wright of Nelson County, son of William Wright (Amherst County)
same	.53			
same	.45			
same	.26	7.05		
William Wright	2.91	2.91		William Wright, Jr., son of William Wright (Amherst County)
Jesse Wright	1.24			1850 Jesse Wright of Nelson County, son of 1799 Benjamin Wright of Amherst County and grandson of 1767 Francis Wright of Amherst County
same	.06	1.30		
Moses Wright	.30			1830 Moses Wright of Amherst County, son of 1799 Benjamin Wright of Amherst County and grandson of 1767 Francis Wright of Amherst County
same	.03			
same	.19	.52		

Appendix: Nelson County, Virginia, 1819 Land Tax List:

Names of Owners	Residence of Owner	Estate	Number of Town Lots	Name of Town	Yearly rent or Value	Amount of Tax on Lots	Number Acres of Land	Description of Land	Distance and bearing from the Court House	Rate of Land pr Acre	Total Amount of Value of Land
The Estate of Jordan Wright	Nelson	fee					138	on the Waters of Tye River adj. S. Edmunds	S 9 M	1.04	143.52
Benjamin Wright	Nelson	fee					46-1/3	on the waters of Rockfish adj Jno W Harris	N 5 M	1.38	6.24

Appendix: Nelson County, Virginia, 1819 Land Tax List:

Names of Owners [continued from prior page]	Total Tax on Land	Total Tax on lots and Land	Explanation of all alterations during the preceeding year	Identification
The Estate of Jordan Wright	1.08	1.08		Estate of 1804 Jordan Wright of Amherst County, son of Parmenos Wright
Benjamin Wright	.46	.46	From John W. H_	1861 Benjamin Wright of Nelson County, son of 1816 Andrew Wright of Nelson County and grandson of William Wright (Amherst County)

1820 LAND TAX LIST

NELSON COUNTY, VIRGINIA

Appendix: Nelson County, Virginia, 1820 Land Tax List:

District of Nelson Andon:

Name of Owner	Residence	Estate	Number of Acres of Land	Description of the Land	Distance and bearing from the Court House	Rate of the land pr acre D C	amt of ____ ____ D C
James Wright	Nelson	Fee	422	Adjoining William H Shelton	N 3 Miles	8.00	3376.00
John Wright (Son of Robert	Nelson "	Fee "	181 111	Adjoining John Melton "	N 1 M N 2 M	12.00 2.00	21.72 2.22
Estate of Andrew Wright	Nelson	Fee	352	Adjoining William Wright	N 4 Miles	8.98	2160.96
William Wright	Nelson	Fee	166	Adjoining Estate of Andrew Wright	N 4 Miles	11.80	1958.80
Jesse Wright	Nelson	Fee	130	Adjoining John Camden	W 17 Miles	9.00	1170.00
Estate of Jordan Wright	Nelson	Fee	138	Adjoining Samuel Edmonds	S 9 Miles	5.00	690.00
John Wright	Nelson	Fee	8½	Adjoining The Town of Lexington	SW	.30	255.00

Appendix: Nelson County, Virginia, 1820 Land Tax List:

District of Nelson Andon:

Name of Owner [continued from prior page]	Amount of tax on the land	Explanation	year	Identification
James Wright	4.22			1839 James Wright of Nelson County, son of William Wright (Amherst County)
John Wright (Son of Robert	2.72 .28	from John McAlexander		John Wright, son of 1816 Robert Wright of Nelson County and grandson of William Wright (Amherst County)
Estate of Andrew Wright	3.95			Estate of 1816 Andrew Wright of Nelson County, son of William Wright (Amherst County)
William Wright	2.45			William Wright, Jr., son of William Wright (Amherst County)
Jesse Wright	1.47			1850 Jesse Wright of Nelson County, son of 1799 Benjamin Wright of Amherst County and grandson of 1767 Francis Wright of Amherst County
Estate of Jordan Wright	.87			Estate of 1804 Jordan Wright of Amherst County, son of Parmenos Wright
John Wright	.32			John Wright, son of 1839 James Wright of Nelson County and grandson of William Wright (Amherst County)

1821 LAND TAX LIST

NELSON COUNTY, VIRGINIA

Appendix: Nelson County, Virginia, 1821 Land Tax List:

District of Nelson Anderson:

Name of owner	Residence	Estate	Number of Acres of land	Description of the land	Distance and bearing from the Court House	Rate of land pr acre	Sums added to the land on account of the building	Total Value of the land
James Wright	Nelson	Fee	422	Adjoining William H Shelton	N 3 Miles	8.00		3376.80
Estate of Andrew Wright	Nelson	Fee	352	Adjoining William Wright	N 4 Miles	8.98	400.00	3160.96
William Wright	Nelson	Fee	166	Adjoining Estate of Andrew Wright	NW 4 Miles	11.80	300.00	1958.80
Jesse Wright	Nelson	Fee	130	Adjoining John Camden	W 17 Miles	9.00		1170.00
Estate of Jordan Wright	Nelson	Fee	138	Adjoining Samuel Edmonds	S 9 Miles	5.00		690.00
John Wright (BS)	Nelson	Fee	8½	Adjoining Lexington	SW	.30		255.00

Appendix: Nelson County, Virginia, 1821 Land Tax List:

District of Nelson Anderson:

Name of owner [continued from prior page]	Amount of tax on the land at p acre	Explanation of alterations during the preceding year	Identification
James Wright	3.44		1839 James Wright of Nelson County, son of William Wright (Amherst County)
Estate of Andrew Wright	2.75		Estate of 1816 Andrew Wright of Nelson County, son of William Wright (Amherst County)
William Wright	1.77		William Wright, Jr., son of William Wright (Amherst County)
Jesse Wright	1.06		1850 Jesse Wright of Nelson County, son of 1799 Benjamin Wright of Amherst County and grandson of 1767 Francis Wright of Amherst County
Estate of Jordan Wright	.63		Estate of 1804 Jordan Wright of Amherst County, son of Parmenos Wright
John Wright (BS)	.24		John Wright, son of 1839 James Wright of Nelson County and grandson of William Wright (Amherst County)

1822 LAND TAX LIST

NELSON COUNTY, VIRGINIA

Appendix: Nelson County, Virginia, 1822 Land Tax List:

District of Nelson Anderson:

Owners Names	Residence	Estate	Number of Acres of land	Description of the land	Distance and bearing from the Court House	Rate of the land pr acre D C	Total value of the buildings	Total value of the land including the buildings
James Wright	Nelson	Fee	422	Adjoining William H Shelton	N 3 Miles	8.00		3376.00
Estate of Andrew Wright	Nelson	Fee	352	Adjoining William Wright	N 4 Miles	8.98	400.00	3160.96
William Wright	Nelson	Fee	166	Adjoining Estate of Andrew Wright	NW 4 Miles	11.80	300.00	1958.80
Jesse Wright	Nelson	Fee	130	Adjoining John Camden	W 17 Miles	9.00		1170.00
Estate of Jordan Wright	Nelson	Fee	138	Adjoining Estate of Samuel Edmonds	S 9 Miles	5.00		690.00
John Wright (BS)	Nelson	Fee	8½	Adjoining the Town of Lexington	SW	.30		255.00
Austin Wright	Nelson	Fee	240	Adjoining John W Murray and Others	S 12 Miles	7.00		1680.00

Appendix: Nelson County, Virginia, 1822 Land Tax List:

District of Nelson Anderson:

Owners Names [continued from prior page]	Total amount of Tax on the land D D	Explanation of alterations during the preceding year	Identification
James Wright	3.04		1839 James Wright of Nelson County, son of William Wright (Amherst County)
Estate of Andrew Wright	2.75		Estate of 1816 Andrew Wright of Nelson County, son of William Wright (Amherst County)
William Wright	1.77		William Wright, Jr., son of William Wright (Amherst County)
Jesse Wright	1.06		1850 Jesse Wright of Nelson County, son of 1799 Benjamin Wright of Amherst County and grandson of 1767 Francis Wright of Amherst County
Estate of Jordan Wright	.63		Estate of 1804 Jordan Wright of Amherst County, son of Parmenos Wright
John Wright	.24		John Wright, son of 1839 James Wright of Nelson County and grandson of William Wright (Amherst County)
Austin Wright	1.52	from Charles Irving and Wife	1838 Augustine Wright of Nelson County, son of 1776 Augustine Wright of Amherst County

1823 LAND TAX LIST

NELSON COUNTY, VIRGINIA

Appendix: Nelson County, Virginia, 1823 Land Tax List:

District of Nelson Anderson:

Name of Owner	Residence	Estate	Number of Acres of land	Description of the land	Distance and bearing from the Court House	Rate of the land pr acre D C	Total value of Buildings	Total value of the land including buildings
James Wright	Nelson	Fee	422	Adjoining William H Shelton	N 3 Miles	8.00		3376.00
Estate of Andrew Wright	Nelson	Fee	352	Adjoining William Wright	N 4 Miles	8.98	400.00	3160.96
William Wright	Nelson	Fee	166	Adjoining Estate of Andrew Wright	NW 4 Miles	11.80	300.00	1958.00
Jesse Wright	Nelson	Fee	130	Adjoining John Camden	W 17 Miles	9.00		1170.00
Estate of Jordan Wright	Nelson	Fee	138	Adjoining Estate of Samuel Edmonds	S 9 Miles	5.00		690.00
John Wright (BS)	Nelson	Fee	8½	Adjoining Town of Lexington	SW	.30		255.00
Austin Wright	Nelson	Fee	240	Adjoining W Murray and Others	S 12 Miles	7.00		1680.00

Appendix: Nelson County, Virginia, 1823 Land Tax List:

District of Nelson Anderson:

Name of owner [continued from prior page]	Total amount of Tax on the land D C	Explanation and alterations during the preceding year	Identification
James Wright	2.71		1839 James Wright of Nelson County, son of William Wright (Amherst County)
Estate of Andrew Wright	2.53		Estate of 1816 Andrew Wright of Nelson County, son of William Wright (Amherst County)
William Wright	1.57		William Wright, Jr., son of William Wright (Amherst County)
Jesse Wright	.94		1850 Jesse Wright of Nelson County, son of 1799 Benjamin Wright of Amherst County and grandson of 1767 Francis Wright of Amherst County
Estate of Jordan Wright	.56		Estate of 1804 Jordan Wright of Amherst County, son of Parmenos Wright
John Wright (BS)	.21		John Wright, son of 1839 James Wright of Nelson County and grandson of William Wright (Amherst County)
Austin Wright	1.35		1838 Augustine Wright of Nelson County, son of 1776 Augustine Wright of Amherst County

1824 LAND TAX LIST

NELSON COUNTY, VIRGINIA

Appendix: Nelson County, Virginia, 1824 Land Tax List:

District of Nelson Anderson:

Names of Owners	Residence			Description of the land	Distance & bearing from the Court House	Rate of land p acre	Total value of the Buildings	Total Value of the Land including Buildings
James Wright	Nelson	Fee	422	Adjoining William H Shelton	N 3 Miles	8.00		33.76
Est Andrew Wright	Nelson	Fee	352	Adjoining Wm Wright	N 4 Miles	8.98	400.00	3160.96
William Wright	Nelson	Fee	166	Adjoining Est Andrew Wright	NW 4 Miles	11.80	300.00	1958.80
Jesse Wright	Nelson	Fee	130	Adjoining John Camden	W 17 Miles	9.00		1170.00
Est Jordan Wright	Nelson	Fee	138	Adjoining Est Saml Edmonds	S 9 Miles	5.00		690.00
John Wright (BS)	Nelson	Fee	8½	Adjoining Town of Lexington	SW	.30		255.00
Austin Wright	Nelson	Fee	240	Adjoining John W Murray & Others	S 12 Miles	7.00		1680.00

Appendix: Nelson County, Virginia, 1824 Land Tax List:

District of Nelson Anderson:

Names of Owners [continued from prior page]	Total amt of Tax on the Land	Explanation and Alterations during the preceding Year	Identification
James Wright	2.71		1839 James Wright of Nelson County, son of William Wright (Amherst County)
Estate of Andrew Wright	2.53		Estate of 1816 Andrew Wright of Nelson County, son of William Wright (Amherst County)
William Wright	1.57		William Wright, Jr., son of William Wright (Amherst County)
Jesse Wright	.94		1850 Jesse Wright of Nelson County, son of 1799 Benjamin Wright of Amherst County and grandson of 1767 Francis Wright of Amherst County
Estate of Jordan Wright	.56		Estate of 1804 Jordan Wright of Amherst County, son of Parmenos Wright
John Wright (BS)	.21		John Wright, son of 1839 James Wright of Nelson County and grandson of William Wright (Amherst County)
Austin Wright	1.35		1838 Augustine Wright of Nelson County, son of 1776 Augustine Wright of Amherst County

1825 LAND TAX LIST

NELSON COUNTY, VIRGINIA

Appendix: Nelson County, Virginia, 1825 Land Tax List:

District of Nelson Anderson:

Name of owner	Residence	Estate	Number of Acres of land	Description of the land	Distance & bearing from the Court House	Rate of land p Acre D C	Total value of the Buildings	Total value of the land including the buildings D C
James Wright	Nelson	Fee	422	Adjoining Lee W Harris	N 3 Miles	8.00		3376.00
Estate of Andrew Wright	Nelson	Fee	352	Adjoining William Wright	N 4 Miles	8.98	400.00	3160.96
William Wright	Nelson	Fee	80	Adjoining Lee W Harris	N 4 Miles	8.20	300.00	656.00
Jesse Wright	Nelson	Fee	130	Adjoining John Camden	W 17 Miles	9.00		1170.00
Estate of Jordan Wright	Nelson	Fee	138	Adjoining Estate of Samuel Edmonds	S 9 Miles	5.00		690.00
Austin Wright	Nelson	Fee	240	Adjoining Bouling and Thornton	S 12 Miles	7.00		1680.00

Appendix: Nelson County, Virginia, 1825 Land Tax List:

District of Nelson Anderson:

Name of Owner [continued from prior page]	Total amount of Tax on the land	Explanation and alterations during the preceding year	Identification
James Wright	2.71		1839 James Wright of Nelson County, son of William Wright (Amherst County)
Estate of Andrew Wright	2.53		Estate of 1816 Andrew Wright of Nelson County, son of William Wright (Amherst County)
William Wright	.53		William Wright, Jr., son of William Wright (Amherst County)
Jesse Wright	.94		1850 Jesse Wright of Nelson County, son of 1799 Benjamin Wright of Amherst County and grandson of 1767 Francis Wright of Amherst County
Estate of Jordan Wright	.56		Estate of 1804 Jordan Wright of Amherst County, son of Parmenos Wright
Austin Wright	1.35		1838 Augustine Wright of Nelson County, son of 1776 Augustine Wright of Amherst County

1826 LAND TAX LIST

NELSON COUNTY, VIRGINIA

Appendix: Nelson County, Virginia, 1826 Land Tax List:

District of Nelson Anderson:

Name of Owner	Residence	Estate	Number of Acres of land	Description of the land	Distance and bearing from the Court House	Rate of land p Acre D C	Total value of the buildings	Total value of the land including the buildings D C
James Wright	Nelson	Fee	422	Adjoining Lee W Harris	N 3 Miles	8.00		3376.00
"	"	"	50	" Alexander McAlexander	N 4 Miles	3.00		150.00
Estate of Andrew Wright	Nelson	Fee	352	Adjoining William Wright	N 4 Miles	8.98	400.00	3160.96
William Wright	Nelson	Fee	80	Adjoining Lee W Harris	N 4 Miles	8.20	300.00	656.00
Jesse Wright	Nelson	Fee	130	Adjoining John Camden	W 17 Miles	9.00		1170.00
Austin Wright	Nelson	Fee	240	Adjoining Bowlin and Thornton	S 12 Miles	7.84	700.00	1881.60

Appendix: Nelson County, Virginia, 1826 Land Tax List:

District of Nelson Anderson:

Name of Owner [continued from prior page]	Total amount of Tax on the land	Explanation of alterations during the preceding year	Identification
James Wright	2.71		1839 James Wright of Nelson County, son of William Wright (Amherst County)
	.12	From Alexander McAlexander	
Estate of Andrew Wright	2.53		Estate of 1816 Andrew Wright of Nelson County, son of William Wright (Amherst County)
William Wright	.53		William Wright, Jr., son of William Wright (Amherst County)
Jesse Wright	.94		1850 Jesse Wright of Nelson County, son of 1799 Benjamin Wright of Amherst County and grandson of 1767 Francis Wright of Amherst County
Austin Wright	1.51		1838 Augustine Wright of Nelson County, son of 1776 Augustine Wright of Amherst County

1827 LAND TAX LIST

NELSON COUNTY, VIRGINIA

Appendix: Nelson County, Virginia, 1827 Land Tax List:

District of Nelson Anderson:

Name of Owner	Residence	Estate	Number of Acres of land	Description of the land	Distance and bearing from the Court House	Rate of land p Acre D C	Total value of the buildings	Total value of the land including the buildings D C
James Wright	Nelson	Fee	422	Adjoining Lee W Harris	N 3 Miles	8.00		3376.00
"	"	"	50	" Alexander McAlexander	N 4 Miles	3.00		150.00
Estate of Andrew Wright	Nelson	Fee	352	Adjoining William Wright	N 4 Miles	8.98	400.00	3160.96
Jesse Wright	Nelson	Fee	135	____ the waters of ____ River	____	2.12		
"	"	"	130	Adjoining John Camden	W 17 Miles	9.00		1170.00
William Wright	Nelson	Fee	80	Adjoining Lee W Harris	N 4 Miles	8.20	300.00	656.00
Austin Wright	Nelson	Fee	240	Adjoining Bowlin and Thornton	S 12 Miles	7.84	700.00	1881.60

Appendix: Nelson County, Virginia, 1827 Land Tax List:

District of Nelson Anderson:

Name of Owner [continued from prior page]	Total amount of Tax on the land	Explanation of alterations during the preceding year	Identification
James Wright	2.71		1839 James Wright of Nelson County, son of William Wright (Amherst County)
"	.12		
Estate of Andrew Wright	2.53		Estate of 1816 Andrew Wright of Nelson County, son of William Wright (Amherst County)
Jesse Wright	.18	From the Register of the land office	1850 Jesse Wright of Nelson County, son of 1799 Benjamin Wright of Amherst County and grandson of 1767 Francis Wright of Amherst County
"	.94		
William Wright	.54		William Wright, Jr., son of William Wright (Amherst County)
Austin Wright	1.51		1838 Augustine Wright of Nelson County, son of 1776 Augustine Wright of Amherst County

1394(051607)

1828 LAND TAX LIST

NELSON COUNTY, VIRGINIA

Appendix: Nelson County, Virginia, 1828 Land Tax List:

District of Nelson Anderson:

Name of Owner	Residence	Estate	Number of Acres of land	Description of the land	Distance and bearing from the Court House	Rate of land p Acre D C	Value of the buildings	Total value of the land including the buildings D C
James Wright	Nelson	Fee	422	Adjoining Lee W Harris and Others	N 3 Miles	8.00		3378.00
"	"	"	50	" Alexander McAlexander and Others	" 4 "	2.00		150.00
Estate of Andrew Wright	Nelson	Fee	352	Adjoining William Wright and Others	N 4 Miles	8.98	400.00	3160.96
William Wright	Nelson	Fee	80	Adjoining Lee W Harris and Others	N 4 Miles	8.20	300.00	656.00
Jesse Wright	Nelson	Fee	130	Adjoining Estate of John Camden and Others	W 17 Miles	9.00		1170.00
"	"	"	285	A new Grant on the waters of Piney River	NW 23 Miles	.75		213.75
Austin Wright	Nelson	Fee	240	Adjoining Bowlin and Thornton and Others	S 12 Miles	7.84	700.00	1881.60

Appendix: Nelson County, Virginia, 1828 Land Tax List:

District of Nelson Anderson:

Name of Owner [continued from prior page]	Total amount of Tax on the land	Explanation of Alterations during the preceding year	Identification
James Wright	2.71		1839 James Wright of Nelson County, son of William Wright (Amherst County)
"	.12		
Estate of Andrew Wright	2.53		Estate of 1816 Andrew Wright of Nelson County, son of William Wright (Amherst County)
William Wright	.53		William Wright, Jr., son of William Wright (Amherst County)
Jesse Wright	.94		1850 Jesse Wright of Nelson County, son of 1799 Benjamin Wright of Amherst County and grandson of 1767 Francis Wright of Amherst County
"	.18		
Austin Wright	1.51		1838 Augustine Wright of Nelson County, son of 1776 Augustine Wright of Amherst County

1394(051607)

1829 LAND TAX LIST

NELSON COUNTY, VIRGINIA

Appendix: Nelson County, Virginia, 1829 Land Tax List:

District of Nelson Anderson:

Name of Owner	Residence	Estate	Number of Acres of Land	Description of the lands	Distance and bearing from the Court house	Rate of land p Acre D C	Total value of the buildings	Total value of the land including the buildings D C
James Wright	Nelson	Fee	422	Adjoining Lee W Harris & others	N 3 Miles	8.00		3376.00
"	"	"	50	" Alexander McAlexander & others	" 4 "	3.00		150.00
Estate of Andrew Wright	Nelson	Fee	352	Adjoining William Wright & others	N 4 Miles	8.98	400.00	3160.96
Jesse Wright	Nelson	Fee	130	Adjoining Estate of John Camden & others	W 17 Miles	9.00		1170.00
Austin Wright	Nelson	Fee	240	Adjoining Bowling and Thornton & others	S 12 Miles	7.84	200.00	1881.60
George G. Ellis, Shelton, William & Daniel L. Wright	Nelson	Fee	285	A new Grant on the waters of Piney River	N.W. 23 Miles	.75		213.75

Appendix: Nelson County, Virginia, 1829 Land Tax List:

District of Nelson Anderson:

Name of Owner [continued from prior page]	Total amount of Tax on the land	Explanation ____ during the pre_____	Identification
James Wright	2.71		1839 James Wright of Nelson County, son of William Wright (Amherst County)
"	.12		
Estate of Andrew Wright	2.53		Estate of 1816 Andrew Wright of Nelson County, son of William Wright (Amherst County)
Jesse Wright	.94		1850 Jesse Wright of Nelson County, son of 1799 Benjamin Wright of Amherst County and grandson of 1767 Francis Wright of Amherst County
Austin Wright	1.51		1838 Augustine Wright of Nelson County, son of 1776 Augustine Wright of Amherst County
George G. Ellis, Shelton, William & Daniel L. Wright	.18	From Jesse Wright	George G. Wright, son of 1850 Jesse Wright of Nelson County, grandson of 1799 Benjamin Wright of Amherst County, and great grandson of 1767 Francis Wright of Amherst County and 1880 Ellis Wright of Amherst County, son of 1850 Jesse Wright of Nelson County, grandson of 1799 Benjamin Wright of Amherst County, and great grandson of 1767 Francis Wright of Amherst County and 1874 Shelton Wright of Nelson County, son of 1850 Jesse Wright of Nelson County, grandson of 1799 Benjamin Wright of Amherst County, and great grandson of 1767 Francis Wright of Amherst County and 1870 William Wright of Amherst County, son of 1850 Jesse Wright of Nelson County, grandson of 1799 Benjamin Wright of Amherst County, and great grandson of 1767 Francis Wright of Amherst County and 1882 Daniel L. Wright of Amherst County, son of 1850 Jesse Wright of Nelson County, grandson of 1799 Benjamin Wright of Amherst County, and great grandson of 1767 Francis Wright of Amherst County

1830 LAND TAX LIST

NELSON COUNTY, VIRGINIA

Appendix: Nelson County, Virginia, 1830 Land Tax List:

District of George Vughan Jr:

Name of Owner	Residence	Estate	Number of Acres of Land	Description of the Land	Distance and bearing from the Court house	Rate of land per Acre $ ¢	Total value of the buildings $ ¢	Total value of the land including the buildings $ ¢
James Wright	Nelson	Fee	422	Adjoining Lee W Harris & others	N 3 Miles	8.00		3376.00
"	"	"	50	" Alexander McAlexander & others	" 4 "	3.00		150.00
Estate Andrew Wright	Nelson	Fee	352	Adjoining William Wright & others	N 4 Miles	8.98	400.00	3160.96
Jesse Wright	Nelson	Fee	130	Adjoining Est. John Camden & others	W 17 Miles	9.00		1170.00
Austin Wright	Nelson	Fee	240	Adjoining Bolling & Thornton & others	S 12 Miles	7.84	200.00	1881.60
George G. Ellis, Shelton, William & Daniel L. Wright	Nelson	Fee	285	A new grant on the waters of Piney River	N.W. 23 Miles	.75		213.75
John B. Wright	Nelson	Fee	100	Adjoining ____ & others	N.W. 6 Miles	4.00		400.00

Appendix: Nelson County, Virginia, 1830 Land Tax List:

District of George Vaughan Jr:

Name of Owner [continued from prior page]	Total amount of Tax on Land $ ¢	Explanation of alterations during the preceding year	Identification
James Wright	2.71		1839 James Wright of Nelson County, son of William Wright (Amherst County)
"	.12		
Estate Andrew Wright	2.53		Estate of 1816 Andrew Wright of Nelson County, son of William Wright (Amherst County)
Jesse Wright	.94		1850 Jesse Wright of Nelson County, son of 1799 Benjamin Wright of Amherst County and grandson of 1767 Francis Wright of Amherst County
Austin Wright	1.51		1838 Augustine Wright of Nelson County, son of 1776 Augustine Wright of Amherst County
George G. Ellis, Shelton, William & Daniel L. Wright	.18		George G. Wright, son of 1850 Jesse Wright of Nelson County, grandson of 1799 Benjamin Wright of Amherst County, and great grandson of 1767 Francis Wright of Amherst County and 1880 Ellis Wright of Amherst County, son of 1850 Jesse Wright of Nelson County, grandson of 1799 Benjamin Wright of Amherst County, and great grandson of 1767 Francis Wright of Amherst County and 1874 Shelton Wright of Nelson County, son of 1850 Jesse Wright of Nelson County, grandson of 1799 Benjamin Wright of Amherst County, and great grandson of 1767 Francis Wright of Amherst County and 1870 William Wright of Amherst County, son of 1850 Jesse Wright of Nelson County, grandson of 1799 Benjamin Wright of Amherst County, and great grandson of 1767 Francis Wright of Amherst County and 1882 Daniel L. Wright of Amherst County, son of 1850 Jesse Wright of Nelson County, grandson of 1799 Benjamin Wright of Amherst County, and great grandson of 1767 Francis Wright of Amherst County
John B. Wright	.32	From Dunston & Givens	John B. Wright, son of 1861 Benjamin Wright of Nelson County, grandson of 1816 Andrew Wright of Nelson County, and great grandson of William Wright (Amherst County)

1831 LAND TAX LIST

NELSON COUNTY, VIRGINIA

Appendix: Nelson County, Virginia, 1831 Land Tax List:

District of Nathan C. Anderson:

Name of Owner	Residence	Estate	Number of Acres of Land	Description of the Land	Distance & bearing from the Ct House	Rate of land pr Acre D C	Total value of the buildings	Total value of the Land Including the buildings D C
James Wright	Nelson	Fee	422	Adj Lee W Harris & others	N 3 Miles	8.00		3376.00
"	"	"	50	" Alexr McAlexander & others	" 4 "	3.00		150.00
Est Andrew Wright	Nelson	Fee	352	Adj Wm Wright & others	N 4 Miles	8.98	400.00	3160.96
Jesse Wright	Nelson	Fee	130	Adj Est John Camden & others	W 17 Miles	9.00		1170.00
Austin Wright	Nelson	Fee	240	Adj Bowling & Thornton & others	S 12 Miles	7.84	200.00	1881.60
George G. Ellis, Shelton, William & Daniel L. Wright	Nelson	Fee	285	A new Grant on Piney River	NW 23 Miles	.75		213.75
John B. Wright	Nelson	Fee	100	Adj ____ & others	NW 6 Miles	4.00		400.00

Appendix: Nelson County, Virginia, 1831 Land Tax List:

District of Nathan C. Anderson:

Name of Owner [continued from prior page]	Total Amt of Tax on the Land $ ¢	Explanation of Alterations during the preceding Year	Identification
James Wright "	2.71 .12		1839 James Wright of Nelson County, son of William Wright (Amherst County)
Est Andrew Wright	2.53		Estate of 1816 Andrew Wright of Nelson County, son of William Wright (Amherst County)
Jesse Wright	.94		1850 Jesse Wright of Nelson County, son of 1799 Benjamin Wright of Amherst County and grandson of 1767 Francis Wright of Amherst County
Austin Wright	1.51		1838 Augustine Wright of Nelson County, son of 1776 Augustine Wright of Amherst County
George G. Ellis, Shelton, William & Daniel L. Wright	.18		George G. Wright, son of 1850 Jesse Wright of Nelson County, grandson of 1799 Benjamin Wright of Amherst County, and great grandson of 1767 Francis Wright of Amherst County and 1880 Ellis Wright of Amherst County, son of 1850 Jesse Wright of Nelson County, grandson of 1799 Benjamin Wright of Amherst County, and great grandson of 1767 Francis Wright of Amherst County and 1874 Shelton Wright of Nelson County, son of 1850 Jesse Wright of Nelson County, grandson of 1799 Benjamin Wright of Amherst County, and great grandson of 1767 Francis Wright of Amherst County and 1870 William Wright of Amherst County, son of 1850 Jesse Wright of Nelson County, grandson of 1799 Benjamin Wright of Amherst County, and great grandson of 1767 Francis Wright of Amherst County and 1882 Daniel L. Wright of Amherst County, son of 1850 Jesse Wright of Nelson County, grandson of 1799 Benjamin Wright of Amherst County, and great grandson of 1767 Francis Wright of Amherst County
John B. Wright	.32		John B. Wright, son of 1861 Benjamin Wright of Nelson County, grandson of 1816 Andrew Wright of Nelson County, and great grandson of William Wright (Amherst County)

1832 LAND TAX LIST

NELSON COUNTY, VIRGINIA

Appendix: Nelson County, Virginia, 1832 Land Tax List:

District of Nathan C. Anderson:

Name of Owner	Residence	Estate	Number of Acres of Land	Description of the Land	Distance & bearing from the Court House	Rate of land pr Acre D C	Total value of the buildings D C	Total value of the Land Including the Buildings D C
James Wright	Nelson	Fee	422	Adj Lee W Harris & Others	N 3 Miles	8.00		3376.00
"	"	"	50	" Alexr McAlexander & Others	" 4 "	3.00		150.00
Est Andrew Wright	Nelson	Fee	352	Adj Wm Wright & Others	N 4 Miles	8.98	400.00	3160.96
Jesse Wright	Nelson	Fee	130	Adj Est John Camden & Others	W 17 Miles	9.00		1170.00
Austin Wright	Nelson	Fee	240	Adj Bowling & Thornton & Others	S 12 Miles	7.00	200.00	1881.60
Geo G. Ellis, Shelton, William & Daniel L. Wright	Nelson	Fee	285	A New Grant on Piney River	NW 23 Miles	.75		213.75
John B. Wright	Nelson	Fee	100	Adj ____	NW 6 Miles	4.00		400.00

Appendix: Nelson County, Virginia, 1832 Land Tax List:

District of Nathan C. Anderson:

Name of Owner [continued from prior page]	Total Amount of Tax on the Land $ ¢	Explanation of Alterations during the preceding Year	Identification
James Wright	2.71		1839 James Wright of Nelson County, son of William Wright (Amherst County)
"	.12		
Est Andrew Wright	2.53		Estate of 1816 Andrew Wright of Nelson County, son of William Wright (Amherst County)
Jesse Wright	.94		1850 Jesse Wright of Nelson County, son of 1799 Benjamin Wright of Amherst County and grandson of 1767 Francis Wright of Amherst County
Austin Wright	1.51		1838 Augustine Wright of Nelson County, son of 1776 Augustine Wright of Amherst County
George G. Ellis, Shelton, William & Daniel L. Wright	.18		George G. Wright, son of 1850 Jesse Wright of Nelson County, grandson of 1799 Benjamin Wright of Amherst County, and great grandson of 1767 Francis Wright of Amherst County and 1880 Ellis Wright of Amherst County, son of 1850 Jesse Wright of Nelson County, grandson of 1799 Benjamin Wright of Amherst County, and great grandson of 1767 Francis Wright of Amherst County and 1874 Shelton Wright of Nelson County, son of 1850 Jesse Wright of Nelson County, grandson of 1799 Benjamin Wright of Amherst County, and great grandson of 1767 Francis Wright of Amherst County and 1870 William Wright of Amherst County, son of 1850 Jesse Wright of Nelson County, grandson of 1799 Benjamin Wright of Amherst County, and great grandson of 1767 Francis Wright of Amherst County and 1882 Daniel L. Wright of Amherst County, son of 1850 Jesse Wright of Nelson County, grandson of 1799 Benjamin Wright of Amherst County, and great grandson of 1767 Francis Wright of Amherst County
John B. Wright	.32		John B. Wright, son of 1861 Benjamin Wright of Nelson County, grandson of 1816 Andrew Wright of Nelson County, and great grandson of William Wright (Amherst County)

1394(051607)

1833 LAND TAX LIST

NELSON COUNTY, VIRGINIA

Appendix: Nelson County, Virginia, 1833 Land Tax List:

District of Nathan C Anderson:

Name of Owner	Residence	Est	Number of Acres of Land	Description of the Land	Distance and bearing from the C House	Rate of Land pr Acre D C	Total value of the Buildings D C	Total value of the Land including the Buildings D C
James Wright	Nelson	Fee	422	Adj Lee W Harris & Others	N 3 Miles	8.00		3376.00
"	"	"	50	" Alexr McAlexander & Others	" 4 "	3.00		150.00
Est Andrew Wright	Nelson	Fee	352	Adj Wm Wright & Others	N 4 Miles	8.98	400.00	3160.96
Jesse Wright	Nelson	Fee	130	Adj Est John Camden & Others	W 17 Miles	9.00		1170.00
Austin Wright	Nelson	Fee	240	Adj Bowling & Thornton & others	S 12 Miles	7.84	200.00	1881.60
Geo G. Ellis, Shelton, William & Daniel L. Wright	Nelson	Fee	285	A New grant on Piney River	NW 23 Miles	.75		213.75
John B. Wright	Nelson	Fee	100	Adj ____	NW 6 Miles	4.00		400.00

Appendix: Nelson County, Virginia, 1833 Land Tax List:

District of Nathan C Anderson:

Name of Owner [continued from prior page]	Total Amt of Tax on Land $ ¢	Explanations of Alterations during the preceeding Year	Identification
James Wright	2.71		1839 James Wright of Nelson County, son of William Wright (Amherst County)
"	.12		
Est Andrew Wright	2.53		Estate of 1816 Andrew Wright of Nelson County, son of William Wright (Amherst County)
Jesse Wright	.94		1850 Jesse Wright of Nelson County, son of 1799 Benjamin Wright of Amherst County and grandson of 1767 Francis Wright of Amherst County
Austin Wright	1.51		1838 Augustine Wright of Nelson County, son of 1776 Augustine Wright of Amherst County
George G. Ellis, Shelton, William & Daniel L. Wright	.18		George G. Wright, son of 1850 Jesse Wright of Nelson County, grandson of 1799 Benjamin Wright of Amherst County, and great grandson of 1767 Francis Wright of Amherst County and 1880 Ellis Wright of Amherst County, son of 1850 Jesse Wright of Nelson County, grandson of 1799 Benjamin Wright of Amherst County, and great grandson of 1767 Francis Wright of Amherst County and 1874 Shelton Wright of Nelson County, son of 1850 Jesse Wright of Nelson County, grandson of 1799 Benjamin Wright of Amherst County, and great grandson of 1767 Francis Wright of Amherst County and 1870 William Wright of Amherst County, son of 1850 Jesse Wright of Nelson County, grandson of 1799 Benjamin Wright of Amherst County, and great grandson of 1767 Francis Wright of Amherst County and 1882 Daniel L. Wright of Amherst County, son of 1850 Jesse Wright of Nelson County, grandson of 1799 Benjamin Wright of Amherst County, and great grandson of 1767 Francis Wright of Amherst County
John B. Wright	.32		John B. Wright, son of 1861 Benjamin Wright of Nelson County, grandson of 1816 Andrew Wright of Nelson County, and great grandson of William Wright (Amherst County)

Appendix: Nelson County, Virginia, 1833 Land Tax List:

District of Nathan C Anderson:

Name of Owner	Residence	Est	Number of Acres of Land	Description of the Land	Distance and bearing from the C House	Rate of Land pr Acre D C	Total value of the Buildings D C	Total value of the Land including the Buildings D C
Thomas Wright	Nelson	Fee	388	Adj Est John Horsley & Others	S 18 Miles	10.00		3880.00

1394(051607)

Appendix: Nelson County, Virginia, 1833 Land Tax List:

District of Nathan C Anderson:

Name of Owner [continued from prior page]	Total Amt of Tax on Land $ ¢	Explanations of Alterations during the preceeding Year	Identification
Thomas Wright	3.11	from Frederick Cabell __ &c	1842 Thomas Wright of Buckingham County

1394(051607)

1834 LAND TAX LIST

NELSON COUNTY, VIRGINIA

Appendix: Nelson County, Virginia, 1834 Land Tax List:

District of Nathan C Anderson:

Name of Owner	Residence	Estate	Number of Acres of Land	Description of the Land	Distance and bearing from the Ct House	Rate of Land pr Acre D C	Total value of the Buildings	Total value of the Land including the Buildings D C
James Wright	Nelson	Fee	422	Adj Lee W Harris & Others	N 3 Miles	8.00		3376.00
"	"	"	50	" Alexr McAlexander & Others	" 4 "	3.00		150.00
Est Andrew Wright	Nelson	Fee	352	Adj Wm Wright & Others	N 4 Miles	8.98	400.00	3160.96
Jesse Wright	Nelson	Fee	130	Adj Est John Camden & Others	W 17 Miles	9.00		1170.00
Austin Wright	Nelson	Fee	240	Adj Bowling & Thornton & Others	S 12 Miles	7.84	200.00	1881.60
Geo G. Ellis, Shelton, William & Daniel L. Wright	Nelson	Fee	285	A new grant on Piney River	NW 23 Miles	.75		213.75
John B. Wright	Nelson	Fee	100	Adj ____	NW 6 Miles	4.00		400.00
"	"	"	1	Adj Thomas Boswell & others	W 24 "	2.00		.02

Appendix: Nelson County, Virginia, 1834 Land Tax List:

District of Nathan C Anderson:

Name of Owner [continued from prior page]	Total Amt of Tax on Land $ ¢	Explanations of Alterations During the preceeding Year	Identification
James Wright "	2.71 .12		1839 James Wright of Nelson County, son of William Wright (Amherst County)
Est Andrew Wright	2.53		Estate of 1816 Andrew Wright of Nelson County, son of William Wright (Amherst County)
Jesse Wright	.94		1850 Jesse Wright of Nelson County, son of 1799 Benjamin Wright of Amherst County and grandson of 1767 Francis Wright of Amherst County
Austin Wright	1.51		1838 Augustine Wright of Nelson County, son of 1776 Augustine Wright of Amherst County
George G. Ellis, Shelton, William & Danl L. Wright	.18		George G. Wright, son of 1850 Jesse Wright of Nelson County, grandson of 1799 Benjamin Wright of Amherst County, and great grandson of 1767 Francis Wright of Amherst County and 1880 Ellis Wright of Amherst County, son of 1850 Jesse Wright of Nelson County, grandson of 1799 Benjamin Wright of Amherst County, and great grandson of 1767 Francis Wright of Amherst County and 1874 Shelton Wright of Nelson County, son of 1850 Jesse Wright of Nelson County, grandson of 1799 Benjamin Wright of Amherst County, and great grandson of 1767 Francis Wright of Amherst County and 1870 William Wright of Amherst County, son of 1850 Jesse Wright of Nelson County, grandson of 1799 Benjamin Wright of Amherst County, and great grandson of 1767 Francis Wright of Amherst County and 1882 Daniel L. Wright of Amherst County, son of 1850 Jesse Wright of Nelson County, grandson of 1799 Benjamin Wright of Amherst County, and great grandson of 1767 Francis Wright of Amherst County
John B. Wright "	.32 .01	from Est Nathl Clarke	John B. Wright, son of 1861 Benjamin Wright of Nelson County, grandson of 1816 Andrew Wright of Nelson County, and great grandson of William Wright (Amherst County)

Appendix: Nelson County, Virginia, 1834 Land Tax List:

District of Nathan C Anderson:

Name of Owner	Residence	Estate	Number of Acres of Land	Description of the Land	Distance and bearing from the Ct House	Rate of Land pr Acre D C	Total value of the Buildings	Total value of the Land including the Buildings D C
Thomas Wright	Amherst	Fee	388	Adj Est John Horsley & Others	S 18 Miles	10.00		3880.00

Appendix: Nelson County, Virginia, 1834 Land Tax List:

District of Nathan C Anderson:

Name of Owner [continued from prior page]	Total Amt of Tax on Land $ ¢	Explanations of Alterations During the preceeding Year	Identification
Thomas Wright	3.11		1842 Thomas Wright of Buckingham County

1835 LAND TAX LIST

NELSON COUNTY, VIRGINIA

Appendix: Nelson County, Virginia, 1835 Land Tax List:

District of Nathan C Anderson:

Name of Owner	Residence	Estate	Number of Acres of Land	Description of the Land	Distance and bearing from the Ct House	Rate of Land pr Acre D C	Total value of the Buildings D C	Total value of the Land including the Buildings D C
James Wright	Nelson	Fee	422	Adj Lee W Harris & Others	N 3 Miles	8.00		3376.00
"	"	"	50	" Alexr McAlexander & Others	" 4 "	3.00		150.00
Est Andrew Wright	Nelson	Fee	352	Adj Wm Wright & Others	N 4 Miles	8.98	400.00	3160.96
Jesse Wright	Nelson	Fee	130	Adj Est John Camden & Others	W 17 Miles	9.00		1170.00
Austin Wright	Nelson	Fee	240	Adj Robt & E W Hutton & Others	S 12 Miles	7.84	200.00	1881.60
Geo G. Ellis, Shelton, Wm and Daniel L Wright	Nelson	Fee	285	A New Grant On Piney River	NW 23 Miles	.75		213.75
John B. Wright	Nelson	Fee	1	Adj Thomas Boswell & Others	W 24 "	2.00		2.00

Appendix: Nelson County, Virginia, 1835 Land Tax List:

District of Nathan C Anderson:

Name of Owner [continued from prior page]	Total Amt of Tax on the Land $ ¢	Explanations of Alterations during the preceeding Year	Identification
James Wright "	2.71 .12		1839 James Wright of Nelson County, son of William Wright (Amherst County)
Est Andrew Wright	2.53		Estate of 1816 Andrew Wright of Nelson County, son of William Wright (Amherst County)
Jesse Wright	.94		1850 Jesse Wright of Nelson County, son of 1799 Benjamin Wright of Amherst County and grandson of 1767 Francis Wright of Amherst County
Austin Wright	1.51		1838 Augustine Wright of Nelson County, son of 1776 Augustine Wright of Amherst County
George G. Ellis, Shelton, Wm and Daniel L Wright	.18		George G. Wright, son of 1850 Jesse Wright of Nelson County, grandson of 1799 Benjamin Wright of Amherst County, and great grandson of 1767 Francis Wright of Amherst County and 1880 Ellis Wright of Amherst County, son of 1850 Jesse Wright of Nelson County, grandson of 1799 Benjamin Wright of Amherst County, and great grandson of 1767 Francis Wright of Amherst County and 1874 Shelton Wright of Nelson County son of 1850 Jesse Wright of Nelson County, grandson of 1799 Benjamin Wright of Amherst County, and great grandson of 1767 Francis Wright of Amherst County and 1870 William Wright of Amherst County, son of 1850 Jesse Wright of Nelson County, grandson of 1799 Benjamin Wright of Amherst County, and great grandson of 1767 Francis Wright of Amherst County and 1882 Daniel L. Wright of Amherst County, son of 1850 Jesse Wright of Nelson County, grandson of 1799 Benjamin Wright of Amherst County, and great grandson of 1767 Francis Wright of Amherst County
John B. Wright	.01		John B. Wright, son of 1861 Benjamin Wright of Nelson County, grandson of 1816 Andrew Wright of Nelson County, and great grandson of William Wright (Amherst County)

Appendix: Nelson County, Virginia, 1835 Land Tax List:

District of Nathan C Anderson:

Name of Owner	Residence	Estate	Number of Acres of Land	Description of the Land	Distance and bearing from the Ct House	Rate of Land pr Acre D C	Total value of the Buildings D C	Total value of the Land including the Buildings D C
Thomas Wright	Nelson	Fee	388	Adj Est John Horsley & Others	S 18 Miles	10.00		3880.00

Appendix: Nelson County, Virginia, 1835 Land Tax List:

District of Nathan C Anderson:

Name of Owner [continued from prior page]	Total Amt of Tax on the Land $ ¢	Explanations of Alterations during the preceeding Year	Identification
Thomas Wright	3.11		1842 Thomas Wright of Buckingham County

1836 LAND TAX LIST

NELSON COUNTY, VIRGINIA

Appendix: Nelson County, Virginia, 1836 Land Tax List:

District of Nathan C Anderson:

Name of Owner	Residence	Estate	Number of Acres of Land	Description of the Land	Distance and bearing from the Court House	Rate of Land per Acre D C	Total value of the Buildings	Total value of the Land including the Buildings D C
James Wright	Nelson	Fee	422	Adj Lee W Harris & Others	N 3 Miles	8.00		3376.00
"	"	"	50	" Alexr McAlexander & Others	" 4 "	3.00		150.00
Est Andrew Wright	Nelson	Fee	352	Adj Wm Wright & Others	N 4 Miles	8.98	400.00	3160.96
Jesse Wright	Nelson	Fee	130	Adj Est John Camden & Others	W 17 Miles	9.00		1170.00
Austin Wright	Nelson	Fee	240	Adj Robt & E W Hutton & Others	S 12 Miles	7.84	200.00	1881.60
George G. Ellis, Shelton, William and Daniel L Wright	Nelson	Fee	285	A New grant on Piney River	NW 23 Miles	.75		213.75
John B. Wright	Nelson	Fee	1	Adj Thomas Boswell & Others	W 24 "	2.00		2.00

Appendix: Nelson County, Virginia, 1836 Land Tax List:

District of Nathan C Anderson:

Name of Owner [continued from prior page]	Total Amount of Tax on Land $ ¢	Identification
James Wright	2.71	1839 James Wright of Nelson County, son of William Wright (Amherst County)
"	.12	
Est Andrew Wright	2.53	Estate of 1816 Andrew Wright of Nelson County, son of William Wright (Amherst County)
Jesse Wright	.94	1850 Jesse Wright of Nelson County, son of 1799 Benjamin Wright of Amherst County and grandson of 1767 Francis Wright of Amherst County
Austin Wright	1.51	1838 Augustine Wright of Nelson County, son of 1776 Augustine Wright of Amherst County
George G. Ellis, Shelton, William and Daniel L Wright	.18	George G. Wright, son of 1850 Jesse Wright of Nelson County, grandson of 1799 Benjamin Wright of Amherst County, and great grandson of 1767 Francis Wright of Amherst County and 1880 Ellis Wright of Amherst County, son of 1850 Jesse Wright of Nelson County, grandson of 1799 Benjamin Wright of Amherst County, and great grandson of 1767 Francis Wright of Amherst County and 1874 Shelton Wright of Nelson County, son of 1850 Jesse Wright of Nelson County, grandson of 1799 Benjamin Wright of Amherst County, and great grandson of 1767 Francis Wright of Amherst County and 1870 William Wright of Amherst County, son of 1850 Jesse Wright of Nelson County, grandson of 1799 Benjamin Wright of Amherst County, and great grandson of 1767 Francis Wright of Amherst County and 1882 Daniel L. Wright of Amherst County, son of 1850 Jesse Wright of Nelson County, grandson of 1799 Benjamin Wright of Amherst County, and great grandson of 1767 Francis Wright of Amherst County
John B. Wright	.01	John B. Wright, son of 1861 Benjamin Wright of Nelson County, grandson of 1816 Andrew Wright of Nelson County, and great grandson of William Wright (Amherst County)

1394(051607)

Appendix: Nelson County, Virginia, 1836 Land Tax List:

District of Nathan C Anderson:

Name of Owner	Residence	Estate	Number of Acres of Land	Description of the Land	Distance and bearing from the Court House	Rate of Land per Acre D C	Total value of the Buildings	Total value of the Land including the Buildings D C
Thomas Wright	Nelson	Fee	388	Adj Est John Horsley & Others	S 18 Miles	10.00		3880.00
George G Wright	Nelson	Fee	6½	On Piny River	W 18 Miles	2.00		13.00

Appendix: Nelson County, Virginia, 1836 Land Tax List:

District of Nathan C Anderson:

Name of Owner [continued from prior page]	Total Amount of Tax on Land $ ¢		Identification
Thomas Wright	3.11		1842 Thomas Wright of Buckingham County
George G. Wright	.02	A New Grant	George G. Wright, son of 1850 Jesse Wright of Nelson County, grandson of 1799 Benjamin Wright of Amherst County, and great grandson of 1767 Francis Wright of Amherst County

1837 LAND TAX LIST

NELSON COUNTY, VIRGINIA

Appendix: Nelson County, Virginia, 1837 Land Tax List:

District of Nathan C Anderson:

Name of Owner	Residence	Estate	Number of Acres of Land	Description of the Land	Distance and bearing from the Ct House	Rate of Land pr Acre D C	Total value of the Buildings D C	Total Value of the Land including the Buildings D C
James Wright	Nelson	Fee	422	Adj Lee W Harris & Others	N 3 Miles	8.00		33.76
"	"	"	50	" Alexr McAlexr & Others	" 4 "	3.00		1.50
Est Andrew Wright	Nelson	Fee	352	Adj Wm Wright & Others	N 4 Miles	8.98	400.00	3160.96
Jesse Wright	Nelson	Fee	130	Adj Est John Camden & Others	W 17 Miles	9.00		1170.00
Austin Wright	Nelson	Fee	240	Adj R Y Hutton & Others	S 12 Miles	7.84	200.00	1881.60
George G. Ellis, Shelton, Wm and Danl L Wright	Nelson	Fee	285	A new grant on Piney River	NW 23 Miles	.75		213.75
John B. Wright	Nelson	Fee	1	Adj Thomas Doswell & Others	W 24 Miles	2.00		2.00

1394(051607)

Appendix: Nelson County, Virginia, 1837 Land Tax List:

District of Nathan C Anderson:

Name of Owner [continued from prior page]	Total Amount of Tax on Land $ ¢	Identification
James Wright "	2.71 .12	1839 James Wright of Nelson County, son of William Wright (Amherst County)
Est Andrew Wright	2.53	Estate of 1816 Andrew Wright of Nelson County, son of William Wright (Amherst County)
Jesse Wright	.94	1850 Jesse Wright of Nelson County, son of 1799 Benjamin Wright of Amherst County and grandson of 1767 Francis Wright of Amherst County
Austin Wright	1.51	1838 Augustine Wright of Nelson County, son of 1776 Augustine Wright of Amherst County
George G. Ellis, Shelton, Wm and Danl L Wright	.18	George G. Wright, son of 1850 Jesse Wright of Nelson County, grandson of 1799 Benjamin Wright of Amherst County, and great grandson of 1767 Francis Wright of Amherst County and 1880 Ellis Wright of Amherst County, son of 1850 Jesse Wright of Nelson County, grandson of 1799 Benjamin Wright of Amherst County, and great grandson of 1767 Francis Wright of Amherst County and 1874 Shelton Wright of Nelson County, son of 1850 Jesse Wright of Nelson County, grandson of 1799 Benjamin Wright of Amherst County, and great grandson of 1767 Francis Wright of Amherst County and 1870 William Wright of Amherst County, son of 1850 Jesse Wright of Nelson County, grandson of 1799 Benjamin Wright of Amherst County, and great grandson of 1767 Francis Wright of Amherst County and 1882 Daniel L. Wright of Amherst County, son of 1850 Jesse Wright of Nelson County, grandson of 1799 Benjamin Wright of Amherst County, and great grandson of 1767 Francis Wright of Amherst County
John B. Wright	.01	John B. Wright, son of 1861 Benjamin Wright of Nelson County, grandson of 1816 Andrew Wright of Nelson County, and great grandson of William Wright (Amherst County)

Appendix: Nelson County, Virginia, 1837 Land Tax List:

District of Nathan C Anderson:

Name of Owner	Residence	Estate	Number of Acres of Land	Description of the Land	Distance and bearing from the Ct House	Rate of Land pr Acre D C	Total value of the Buildings D C	Total Value of the Land including the Buildings D C
Thomas Wright	Nelson	Fee	388	Adj Est John Horsley & Others	S 18 Miles	10.00		3880.00
George G Wright	Nelson	Fee	6½	On Piny River	W 18 Miles	2.00		13.00
Shelton Wright	Nelson	Fee	300	Adj Saml McD Reese & others	W 15 Miles	8.33	400.00	2499.00

Appendix: Nelson County, Virginia, 1837 Land Tax List:

District of Nathan C Anderson:

Name of Owner [continued from prior page]	Total Amount of Tax on Land $ ¢		Identification
Thomas Wright	3.11		1842 Thomas Wright of Buckingham County
George G. Wright	.02	A New Grant	George G. Wright, son of 1850 Jesse Wright of Nelson County, grandson of 1799 Benjamin Wright of Amherst County, and great grandson of 1767 Francis Wright of Amherst County
Shelton Wright	2.00	from George Jones	1874 Shelton Wright of Nelson County, son of 1850 Jesse Wright of Nelson County, grandson of 1799 Benjamin Wright of Amherst County, and great grandson of 1767 Francis Wright of Amherst County

1394(051607)

1838 LAND TAX LIST

NELSON COUNTY, VIRGINIA

Appendix: Nelson County, Virginia, 1838 Land Tax List:

District of Nathan C Anderson:

Name of Owner	Residence	Estate	Number of Acres	Who Adjoining	Distance and bearing from the Court House	Value of Land pr Acre D C	Total Value of the Buildings D C	Total Value of the Land including the Buildings D C
James Wright	Nelson	Fee	422	Adj Est Lee W Harris & Others	N 3 Miles	8.00		3376.00
"	"	"	50	" Alexr McAlexander & Others	" 4 "	3.00		150.00
Est Andrew Wright	Nelson	Fee	352	Adj Wm Wright & Others	N 4 Miles	8.98	400.00	3160.96
Jesse Wright	Nelson	Fee	130	Adj Est John Camden & Others	W 17 Miles	9.00		1170.00
Austin Wright	Nelson	Fee	240	Adj Robert T Hubbard & Others	S 12 Miles	7.84	200.00	1881.60
George G. Ellis, Shelton, William and Daniel L Wright	Nelson	Fee	285	A New Grant on Piney River	NW 23 Miles	.75		213.75
John B. Wright	Nelson	Fee	1	Adj Thomas Doswell & Others	W 24	2.00		2.00

1394(051607)

Appendix: Nelson County, Virginia, 1838 Land Tax List:

District of Nathan C Anderson:

Name of Owner [continued from prior page]	Total Amount of Tax on Land $ ¢	Identification
James Wright	3.38	1839 James Wright of Nelson County, son of William Wright (Amherst County)
"	.15	
Est Andrew Wright	3.16	Estate of 1816 Andrew Wright of Nelson County, son of William Wright (Amherst County)
Jesse Wright	1.17	1850 Jesse Wright of Nelson County, son of 1799 Benjamin Wright of Amherst County and grandson of 1767 Francis Wright of Amherst County
Austin Wright	1.89	1838 Augustine Wright of Nelson County, son of 1776 Augustine Wright of Amherst County
George G. Ellis, Shelton, William and Daniel L Wright	.22	George G. Wright, son of 1850 Jesse Wright of Nelson County, grandson of 1799 Benjamin Wright of Amherst County, and great grandson of 1767 Francis Wright of Amherst County and 1880 Ellis Wright of Amherst County, son of 1850 Jesse Wright of Nelson County, grandson of 1799 Benjamin Wright of Amherst County, and great grandson of 1767 Francis Wright of Amherst County and 1874 Shelton Wright of Nelson County, son of 1850 Jesse Wright of Nelson County, grandson of 1799 Benjamin Wright of Amherst County, and great grandson of 1767 Francis Wright of Amherst County and 1870 William Wright of Amherst County, son of 1850 Jesse Wright of Nelson County, grandson of 1799 Benjamin Wright of Amherst County, and great grandson of 1767 Francis Wright of Amherst County and 1882 Daniel L. Wright of Amherst County, son of 1850 Jesse Wright of Nelson County, grandson of 1799 Benjamin Wright of Amherst County, and great grandson of 1767 Francis Wright of Amherst County
John B. Wright	.01	John B. Wright, son of 1861 Benjamin Wright of Nelson County, grandson of 1816 Andrew Wright of Nelson County, and great grandson of William Wright (Amherst County)

Appendix: Nelson County, Virginia, 1838 Land Tax List:

District of Nathan C Anderson:

Name of Owner	Residence	Estate	Number of Acres	Who Adjoining	Distance and bearing from the Court House	Value of Land pr Acre D C	Total Value of the Buildings D C	Total Value of the Land including the Buildings D C
Thomas Wright	Nelson	Fee	388	Adj Est John Horsley & Others	S 18 Miles	10.00		3880.00
George G Wright	Nelson	Fee	6½	On Piny River	W 18 Miles	2.00		13.00
Shelton Wright	Nelson	Fee	300	Adj Saml McD Reid & Others	W 15 Miles	8.33	400.00	2499.00

Appendix: Nelson County, Virginia, 1838 Land Tax List:

District of Nathan C Anderson:

Name of Owner [continued from prior page]	Total Amount of Tax on Land $ ¢	Identification
Thomas Wright	3.88	1842 Thomas Wright of Buckingham County
George G. Wright	.02	George G. Wright, son of 1850 Jesse Wright of Nelson County, grandson of 1799 Benjamin Wright of Amherst County, and great grandson of 1767 Francis Wright of Amherst County
Shelton Wright	2.50	1874 Shelton Wright of Nelson County, son of 1850 Jesse Wright of Nelson County, grandson of 1799 Benjamin Wright of Amherst County, and great grandson of 1767 Francis Wright of Amherst County

1839 LAND TAX LIST

NELSON COUNTY, VIRGINIA

Appendix: Nelson County, Virginia, 1839 Land Tax List:

District of Nathan C Anderson:

Name of Owner	Residence	Estate	Number of Acres of Land	Description of the Land	Distance and bearing from the Court House	Rate of Land pr Acre D C	Total Value of the Buildings D C	Total Value of the Land including the Buildings D C
James Wright	Nelson	Fee	422	Adj Est Lee W Harris & Others	N 3 M	8.00		3376.00
"	"	"	50	" Alexr McAlexander & Others	" 4 "	3.00		150.00
Est Andrew Wright	Nelson	Fee	352	Adj Est Lee W Harris & Others	N 4 M	8.98	400.00	3160.96
Jesse Wright	Nelson	Fee	130	Adj Est John Camden & Others	W 17 M	9.00		1170.00
George G. Shelton William and Daniel L Wright	Nelson	Fee	285	A New Grant on Piny River	NW 23 M	.75		213.75
John B. Wright	Nelson	Fee	1	Adj Thomas Doswell & Others	W 24 "	2.00		2.00
Thomas Wright	Nelson	Fee	388	Adj Est John Horsley & Others	S 18 M	10.00		3880.00

Appendix: Nelson County, Virginia, 1839 Land Tax List:

District of Nathan C Anderson:

Name of Owner [continued from prior page]	Total Amount of Tax on Land $ ¢	Identification
James Wright	3.38	1839 James Wright of Nelson County, son of William Wright (Amherst County)
"	.15	
Est Andrew Wright	3.17	Estate of 1816 Andrew Wright of Nelson County, son of William Wright (Amherst County)
Jesse Wright	1.17	1850 Jesse Wright of Nelson County, son of 1799 Benjamin Wright of Amherst County and grandson of 1767 Francis Wright of Amherst County
George G. Shelton, William and Daniel L Wright	.22	George G. Wright, son of 1850 Jesse Wright of Nelson County, grandson of 1799 Benjamin Wright of Amherst County, and great grandson of 1767 Francis Wright of Amherst County and 1874 Shelton Wright of Nelson County, son of 1850 Jesse Wright of Nelson County, grandson of 1799 Benjamin Wright of Amherst County, and great grandson of 1767 Francis Wright of Amherst County and 1870 William Wright of Amherst County, son of 1850 Jesse Wright of Nelson County, grandson of 1799 Benjamin Wright of Amherst County, and great grandson of 1767 Francis Wright of Amherst County and 1882 Daniel L. Wright of Amherst County, son of 1850 Jesse Wright of Nelson County, grandson of 1799 Benjamin Wright of Amherst County, and great grandson of 1767 Francis Wright of Amherst County
John B. Wright	.01	John B. Wright, son of 1861 Benjamin Wright of Nelson County, grandson of 1816 Andrew Wright of Nelson County, and great grandson of William Wright (Amherst County)
Thomas Wright	3.88	1842 Thomas Wright of Buckingham County

Appendix: Nelson County, Virginia, 1839 Land Tax List:

District of Nathan C Anderson:

Name of Owner	Residence	Estate	Number of Acres of Land	Description of the Land	Distance and bearing from the Court House	Rate of Land pr Acre D C	Total Value of the Buildings D C	Total Value of the Land including the Buildings D C
George G Wright	Nelson	Fee	6½	On Piny River & Others	W 18 M	2.00		13.00
Shelton Wright	Nelson	Fee	300	Adj Saml McD Reid & Others	W 15 M	8.33	400.00	2499.00

Appendix: Nelson County, Virginia, 1839 Land Tax List:

District of Nathan C Anderson:

Name of Owner [continued from prior page]	Total Amount of Tax on Land $ ¢	Identification
George G. Wright	.02	George G. Wright, son of 1850 Jesse Wright of Nelson County, grandson of 1799 Benjamin Wright of Amherst County, and great grandson of 1767 Francis Wright of Amherst County
Shelton Wright	2.50	1874 Shelton Wright of Nelson County, son of 1850 Jesse Wright of Nelson County, grandson of 1799 Benjamin Wright of Amherst County, and great grandson of 1767 Francis Wright of Amherst County

1840 LAND TAX LIST

NELSON COUNTY, VIRGINIA

Appendix: Nelson County, Virginia, 1840 Land Tax List:

District of John H Wingfield:

Names of Owners	Residence	Estate	Number of Acres of land	Description of the Land	Distance and Bearing from the Court House	Value of land pr Acre	Total Value of the Buildings	Total Value of land including the Buildings
Est James Wright	Nelson	Fee	422	Adjonig Est Lee W Harris & others	N 5 Miles	7.94	400.00	3350.68
"	"	"	50	" Alexr McAlexander & others	" "	8.00		100.00
Est Andrew Wright	Nelson	Fee	352	Adjoing William Wright & others	N 6 Miles	7.10	400.00	2499.20
Jesse Wright	Nelson	Fee	130	Adjoing Benjn Camden & others	W 15 Miles	8.81	300.00	145.35
_ Shelton Wm & Danl L Wright	Nelson	Fee	285	On Piney River	NW 23 Miles	.50		142.40
John B. Wright	Nelson	Fee	1	Adjoing Thomas Doswell & others	W 24 Miles	1.50		1.50
Thomas Wright	Nelson	Fee	357¼	Adjoing Est Jno Horsley & others	S 18 Miles	3.00		1073.25

Appendix: Nelson County, Virginia, 1840 Land Tax List:

District of John H Wingfield:

Names of Owners [continued from prior page]	Total Amount of Tax on land	Identification
Est James Wright	3.36	Estate of 1839 James Wright of Nelson County, son of William Wright (Amherst County)
"	.10	
Est Andrew Wright	2.50	Estate of 1816 Andrew Wright of Nelson County, son of William Wright (Amherst County)
Jesse Wright	1.15	1850 Jesse Wright of Nelson County, son of 1799 Benjamin Wright of Amherst County and grandson of 1767 Francis Wright of Amherst County
_ Shelton, Wm & Danl L Wright	.15	George G. Wright, son of 1850 Jesse Wright of Nelson County, grandson of 1799 Benjamin Wright of Amherst County, and great grandson of 1767 Francis Wright of Amherst County and 1874 Shelton Wright of Nelson County, son of 1850 Jesse Wright of Nelson County, grandson of 1799 Benjamin Wright of Amherst County, and great grandson of 1767 Francis Wright of Amherst County and 1870 William Wright of Amherst County, son of 1850 Jesse Wright of Nelson County, grandson of 1799 Benjamin Wright of Amherst County, and great grandson of 1767 Francis Wright of Amherst County and 1882 Daniel L. Wright of Amherst County, son of 1850 Jesse Wright of Nelson County, grandson of 1799 Benjamin Wright of Amherst County, and great grandson of 1767 Francis Wright of Amherst County
John B. Wright	.01	John B. Wright, son of 1861 Benjamin Wright of Nelson County, grandson of 1816 Andrew Wright of Nelson County, and great grandson of William Wright (Amherst County)
Thomas Wright	1.08	1842 Thomas Wright of Buckingham County

Appendix: Nelson County, Virginia, 1840 Land Tax List:

District of John H Wingfield:

Names of Owners	Residence	Estate	Number of Acres of land	Description of the Land	Distance and Bearing from the Court House	Value of land pr Acre	Total Value of the Buildings	Total Value of land including the Buildings
George G Wright	Amherst(?)	Fee	6½	Adjoing On Piny River & others	W 16 Miles	6.50		.42
Shelton Wright	Nelson	Fee	300	Adjoing Saml McD Read & others	SW 15 Miles	5.69	500.00	1701.00

Appendix: Nelson County, Virginia, 1840 Land Tax List:

District of John H Wingfield:

Names of Owners [continued from prior page]	Total Amount of Tax on land	Identification
George G. Wright	.05	George G. Wright, son of 1850 Jesse Wright of Nelson County, grandson of 1799 Benjamin Wright of Amherst County, and great grandson of 1767 Francis Wright of Amherst County
Shelton Wright	1.71	1874 Shelton Wright of Nelson County, son of 1850 Jesse Wright of Nelson County, grandson of 1799 Benjamin Wright of Amherst County, and great grandson of 1767 Francis Wright of Amherst County

1841 LAND TAX LIST

NELSON COUNTY, VIRGINIA

Appendix: Nelson County, Virginia, 1841 Land Tax List:

District of John H Wingfield:

Names of Owners	Residence	Estate	No Acres	Description of the Land	Distance and bearing from the Court House	Value of Land including building	Sum added to Land including building	Total Value of Land and Buildings
Est James Wright	Nelson	Fee	422	adj Est Lee W Harris & others	N 5 miles	7.94	400.00	3350.68
"	"	"	50	" Alexr McAlexander & others	" "	2.00		400.00
Est Andrew Wright	Nelson	Fee	352	adj Eid(?) William Wright	N 6 Miles	7.10	400.00	2494.20
Jesse Wright	Nelson	Fee	130	adj Benjamin Camden & others	W 15 Miles	8.81	300.00	2145.50
_ G Shelton Wm & Daniel L Wright	Nelson	Fee	285	on Piney River & others	SW 23 Miles	.50		142.50
John B. Wright	Nelson	Fee	1	Adjoing Thomas Doswell & others	W 24 Miles	1.50		1.50
Thomas Wright	Nelson	Fee	357¼	adj Est John Horsley & others	S 16 Miles	3.00		1073.25

Appendix: Nelson County, Virginia, 1841 Land Tax List:

District of John H Wingfield:

Names of Owners [continued from prior page]	Amount of Tax on the whole Tract at the legal rate	Explanations	Identification
Est James Wright	4.19		Estate of 1839 James Wright of Nelson County, son of William Wright (Amherst County)
"	.13		
Est Andrew Wright	3.12		Estate of 1816 Andrew Wright of Nelson County, son of William Wright (Amherst County)
Jesse Wright	1.44		1850 Jesse Wright of Nelson County, son of 1799 Benjamin Wright of Amherst County and grandson of 1767 Francis Wright of Amherst County
_ G Shelton Wm & Daniel L Wright	.18		George G. Wright, son of 1850 Jesse Wright of Nelson County, grandson of 1799 Benjamin Wright of Amherst County, and great grandson of 1767 Francis Wright of Amherst County and 1874 Shelton Wright of Nelson County, son of 1850 Jesse Wright of Nelson County, grandson of 1799 Benjamin Wright of Amherst County, and great grandson of 1767 Francis Wright of Amherst County and 1870 William Wright of Amherst County, son of 1850 Jesse Wright of Nelson County, grandson of 1799 Benjamin Wright of Amherst County, and great grandson of 1767 Francis Wright of Amherst County and 1882 Daniel L. Wright of Amherst County, son of 1850 Jesse Wright of Nelson County, grandson of 1799 Benjamin Wright of Amherst County, and great grandson of 1767 Francis Wright of Amherst County
John B. Wright	.01		John B. Wright, son of 1861 Benjamin Wright of Nelson County, grandson of 1816 Andrew Wright of Nelson County, and great grandson of William Wright (Amherst County)
Thomas Wright	1.35		1842 Thomas Wright of Buckingham County

1394(051607)

Appendix: Nelson County, Virginia, 1841 Land Tax List:

District of John H Wingfield:

Names of Owners	Residence	Estate	No Acres	Description of the Land	Distance and bearing from the Court House	Value of Land including building	Sum added to Land including building	Total Value of Land and Buildings
Geo G Wright	Amherst	Fee	6½	on Piny River	W 16 Miles	6.50		42.00
Shelton Wright	Nelson	Fee	300	Adjoing Saml McD Read & others	SW 15 Miles	5.69	500.00	1701.00

Appendix: Nelson County, Virginia, 1841 Land Tax List:

District of John H Wingfield:

Names of Owners [continued from prior page]	Amount of Tax on the whole Tract at the legal rate	Explanations	Identification
Geo G. Wright	.06		George G. Wright, son of 1850 Jesse Wright of Nelson County, grandson of 1799 Benjamin Wright of Amherst County, and great grandson of 1767 Francis Wright of Amherst County
Shelton Wright	2.10		1874 Shelton Wright of Nelson County, son of 1850 Jesse Wright of Nelson County, grandson of 1799 Benjamin Wright of Amherst County, and great grandson of 1767 Francis Wright of Amherst County

1842 LAND TAX LIST

NELSON COUNTY, VIRGINIA

Appendix: Nelson County, Virginia, 1842 Land Tax List:

District of John H Wingfield:

Names of Owners	Residence	Estate	Number of Acres of Land	Description of land	Distance and bearing from the Ct House	Value of land pr acre including Buildings	Sum added to land on account of Buildings	Total Value of the land and Buildings
Est James Wright	Nelson	Fee	422	Adjonig Est Lee W Harris & others	N 5 miles	7.94	400.00	3350.68
"	"	"	50	" Foster S McAlexander & others	" "	2.00		100.00
Est Andrew Wright	Nelson	Fee	352	Adjonig Est Lee W Harris & others	N 6 Miles	7.10	400.00	2694.20
Jesse Wright	Nelson	Fee	130	Adjonig Benjn Camden & others	W 15 Miles	8.81	300.00	1145.30
Geo G Shelton, Wm & D. L. Wright	Nelson	Fee	285	On Piney River	SW 23 Miles	.50		142.50
John B. Wright	Nelson	Fee	1	Adjoing Thomas Doswell & others	W 24 Miles	1.50		1.50
William R Wright	Nelson	Fee	388	On James River	S 18 Miles	3.00		1164.00
George G Wright	unknown	Fee	6½	On Piny River	W 16 Miles	6.50		42.00

Appendix: Nelson County, Virginia, 1842 Land Tax List:

District of John H Wingfield:

Names of Owners [continued from prior page]	Amount of Tax on the whole Tract at the legal rate	Explanation of alterations during the preceeding year	Identification
Est James Wright	4.19		Estate of 1839 James Wright of Nelson County, son of William Wright (Amherst County)
"	.13		
Est Andrew Wright	3.12		Estate of 1816 Andrew Wright of Nelson County, son of William Wright (Amherst County)
Jesse Wright	1.44		1850 Jesse Wright of Nelson County, son of 1799 Benjamin Wright of Amherst County and grandson of 1767 Francis Wright of Amherst County
Geo G Shelton, Wm & D. L. Wright	.18		George G. Wright, son of 1850 Jesse Wright of Nelson County, grandson of 1799 Benjamin Wright of Amherst County, and great grandson of 1767 Francis Wright of Amherst County and 1874 Shelton Wright of Nelson County, son of 1850 Jesse Wright of Nelson County, grandson of 1799 Benjamin Wright of Amherst County, and great grandson of 1767 Francis Wright of Amherst County and 1870 William Wright of Amherst County, son of 1850 Jesse Wright of Nelson County, grandson of 1799 Benjamin Wright of Amherst County, and great grandson of 1767 Francis Wright of Amherst County and 1882 Daniel L. Wright of Amherst County, son of 1850 Jesse Wright of Nelson County, grandson of 1799 Benjamin Wright of Amherst County, and great grandson of 1767 Francis Wright of Amherst County
John B. Wright	.01		John B. Wright, son of 1861 Benjamin Wright of Nelson County, grandson of 1816 Andrew Wright of Nelson County, and great grandson of William Wright (Amherst County)
William R. Wright	1.46	From Thomas Wright	1871 William R. Wright of Buckingham County, son of 1842 Thomas Wright of Buckingham County
George G. Wright	.06		George G. Wright, son of 1850 Jesse Wright of Nelson County, grandson of 1799 Benjamin Wright of Amherst County, and great grandson of 1767 Francis Wright of Amherst County

1394(051607)

Appendix: Nelson County, Virginia, 1842 Land Tax List:

District of John H Wingfield:

Names of Owners	Residence	Estate	Number of Acres of Land	Description of land	Distance and bearing from the Ct House	Value of land pr acre including Buildings	Sum added to land on account of Buildings	Total Value of the land and Buildings
Shelton Wright	Nelson	Fee	300	Adjoing Saml McD Read & others	SW 15 Miles	5.69	500.00	1701.00

Appendix: Nelson County, Virginia, 1842 Land Tax List:

District of John H Wingfield:

Names of Owners [continued from prior page]	Amount of Tax on the whole Tract at the legal rate	Explanation of alterations during the preceeding year	Identification
Shelton Wright	2.13		1874 Shelton Wright of Nelson County, son of 1850 Jesse Wright of Nelson County, grandson of 1799 Benjamin Wright of Amherst County, and great grandson of 1767 Francis Wright of Amherst County

1843 LAND TAX LIST

NELSON COUNTY, VIRGINIA

Appendix: Nelson County, Virginia, 1843 Land Tax List:

District of John H Wingfield:

Names of Owners	Residence	Estate	Number of Acres of Land	Description of land	Distance and Bearing from the Court House	Value of land pr acre including Buildings	Sum added to the land on account of the Buildings	Total Value of the Land and Buildings
Est James Wright	Nelson	Fee	422	Adjoining Est Lee W Harris & others	N 5 miles	7.94	400.00	3350.68
"	"	"	50	" Foster S McAlexander & others	" "	2.00		100.00
Est Andrew Wright	Nelson	Fee	352	Adjoining Est Lee W Harris & others	N 6 Miles	7.10	400.00	2494.20
Jesse Wright	Nelson	Fee	130	Adjoining Benjamin Camden & others	W 15 Miles	8.81	300.00	1145.30
George G Shelton, Wm & D. L. Wright	Nelson	Fee	285	On Piny River	SW 23 Miles	.50		142.50
John B. Wright	Nelson	Fee	1	Adjoining Thomas Doswell & others	W 24 Miles	1.50		1.50
William R Wright	Nelson	Fee	388	On James River	S 18 Miles	3.00		1164.00

Appendix: Nelson County, Virginia, 1843 Land Tax List:

District of John H Wingfield:

Names of Owners [continued from prior page]	Amount of Tax on the whole tract at the legal rate	Explanation of alterations &c	Identification
Est James Wright	5.03		Estate of 1839 James Wright of Nelson County, son of William Wright (Amherst County)
"	.15		
Est Andrew Wright	3.75		Estate of 1816 Andrew Wright of Nelson County, son of William Wright (Amherst County)
Jesse Wright	1.72		1850 Jesse Wright of Nelson County, son of 1799 Benjamin Wright of Amherst County and grandson of 1767 Francis Wright of Amherst County
George G Shelton, Wm & D. L. Wright	.22		George G. Wright, son of 1850 Jesse Wright of Nelson County, grandson of 1799 Benjamin Wright of Amherst County, and great grandson of 1767 Francis Wright of Amherst County and 1874 Shelton Wright of Nelson County, son of 1850 Jesse Wright of Nelson County, grandson of 1799 Benjamin Wright of Amherst County, and great grandson of 1767 Francis Wright of Amherst County and 1870 William Wright of Amherst County, son of 1850 Jesse Wright of Nelson County, grandson of 1799 Benjamin Wright of Amherst County, and great grandson of 1767 Francis Wright of Amherst County and 1882 Daniel L. Wright of Amherst County, son of 1850 Jesse Wright of Nelson County, grandson of 1799 Benjamin Wright of Amherst County, and great grandson of 1767 Francis Wright of Amherst County
John B. Wright	.01		John B. Wright, son of 1861 Benjamin Wright of Nelson County, grandson of 1816 Andrew Wright of Nelson County, and great grandson of William Wright (Amherst County)
William R. Wright	1.75	From Thomas Wright 1842	1871 William R. Wright of Buckingham County, son of 1842 Thomas Wright of Buckingham County

Appendix: Nelson County, Virginia, 1843 Land Tax List:

District of John H Wingfield:

Names of Owners	Residence	Estate	Number of Acres of Land	Description of land	Distance and Bearing from the Court House	Value of land pr acre including Buildings	Sum added to the land on account of the Buildings	Total Value of the Land and Buildings
George G Wright	Unknown	Fee	6½	On Piny River	W 16 Miles	6.50		42.00
Shelton Wright	Nelson	Fee	230	Adjoining Saml McD Read & others	SW 15 Miles	5.69	500.00	1308.70

Appendix: Nelson County, Virginia, 1843 Land Tax List:

District of John H Wingfield:

Names of Owners [continued from prior page]	Amount of Tax on the whole tract at the legal rate	Explanation of alterations &c	Identification
George G. Wright	.07		George G. Wright, son of 1850 Jesse Wright of Nelson County, grandson of 1799 Benjamin Wright of Amherst County, and great grandson of 1767 Francis Wright of Amherst County
Shelton Wright	1.97		1874 Shelton Wright of Nelson County, son of 1850 Jesse Wright of Nelson County, grandson of 1799 Benjamin Wright of Amherst County, and great grandson of 1767 Francis Wright of Amherst County

1844 LAND TAX LIST

NELSON COUNTY, VIRGINIA

Appendix: Nelson County, Virginia, 1844 Land Tax List:

District of John H Wingfield:

Name of Owner	Residence	Estate	Number of acres of land	Description of Land	Distance and bearing from the Court House	Value of land pr acre including Buildings	Sum added to the land on account of the buildings	Total Value of the land including Buildings
Est James Wright	Nelson	Fee	422	Adj Est Lee W Harris & others	N 5 miles	7.94	400.00	3350.68
"	"	"	50	" Foster S McAlexander & others	" "	2.00		100.00
Est Andrew Wright	Nelson	Fee	352	Adj Est Lee W Harris & others	N 6 Miles	7.10	400.00	2494.20
Jesse Wright	Nelson	Fee	130	Adj Benjamin Camden & others	W 15 Miles	8.81	300.00	1145.30
George G Shelton, Wm & D. L. Wright	Nelson	Fee	285	On Piny River	SW 23 Miles	.50		142.50
John B. Wright	Nelson	Fee	1	Adj Thomas Doswell	W 24 Miles	1.50		1.50
William R Wright	Nelson	Fee	388	Adj William Horsely & others	S 18 Miles	3.00		1164.00
George G Wright	unkn	Fee	6½	On Piny River	W 16 Miles	6.50		42.00

Appendix: Nelson County, Virginia, 1844 Land Tax List:

District of John H Wingfield:

Name of Owner [continued from prior page]	Amount of Tax on the whole Tract at the legal rate	Explanation of Alterations	Identification
Est James Wright	4.19		Estate of 1839 James Wright of Nelson County, son of William Wright (Amherst County)
"	.13		
Est Andrew Wright	3.11		Estate of 1816 Andrew Wright of Nelson County, son of William Wright (Amherst County)
Jesse Wright	1.44		1850 Jesse Wright of Nelson County, son of 1799 Benjamin Wright of Amherst County and grandson of 1767 Francis Wright of Amherst County
George G Shelton, Wm & D. L. Wright	.18		George G. Wright, son of 1850 Jesse Wright of Nelson County, grandson of 1799 Benjamin Wright of Amherst County, and great grandson of 1767 Francis Wright of Amherst County and 1874 Shelton Wright of Nelson County son of 1850 Jesse Wright of Nelson County, grandson of 1799 Benjamin Wright of Amherst County, and great grandson of 1767 Francis Wright of Amherst County and 1870 William Wright of Amherst County, son of 1850 Jesse Wright of Nelson County, grandson of 1799 Benjamin Wright of Amherst County, and great grandson of 1767 Francis Wright of Amherst County and 1882 Daniel L. Wright of Amherst County, son of 1850 Jesse Wright of Nelson County, grandson of 1799 Benjamin Wright of Amherst County, and great grandson of 1767 Francis Wright of Amherst County
John B. Wright	.01		John B. Wright, son of 1861 Benjamin Wright of Nelson County, grandson of 1816 Andrew Wright of Nelson County, and great grandson of William Wright (Amherst County)
William R. Wright	1.46		1871 William R. Wright of Buckingham County, son of 1842 Thomas Wright of Buckingham County
George G. Wright	.06		George G. Wright, son of 1850 Jesse Wright of Nelson County, grandson of 1799 Benjamin Wright of Amherst County, and great grandson of 1767 Francis Wright of Amherst County

Appendix: Nelson County, Virginia, 1844 Land Tax List:

District of John H Wingfield:

Name of Owner	Residence	Estate	Number of acres of land	Description of Land	Distance and bearing from the Court House	Value of land pr acre including Buildings	Sum added to the land on account of the buildings	Total Value of the land including Buildings
Shelton Wright	Nelson	Fee	230	Adj Saml McD Read & others	SW 15 Miles	5.69	500.00	1308.70

1394(051607)

Appendix: Nelson County, Virginia, 1844 Land Tax List:

District of John H Wingfield:

Name of Owner [continued from prior page]	Amount of Tax on the whole Tract at the legal rate	Explanation of Alterations	Identification
Shelton Wright	1.64		1874 Shelton Wright of Nelson County, son of 1850 Jesse Wright of Nelson County, grandson of 1799 Benjamin Wright of Amherst County, and great grandson of 1767 Francis Wright of Amherst County

1845 LAND TAX LIST

NELSON COUNTY, VIRGINIA

Appendix: Nelson County, Virginia, 1845 Land Tax List:

District of John H Wingfield:

Name of Owner	Residence	Estate whether held in fee simple for life &c	No. of Acres	Description of the land, as to watercourses, mountains and contiguous tracts	Distance and bearing from the court house	Value of land per acre, including buildings	Sum added to the land on account of buildings	Total value of the land and buildings
Est James Wright	Nelson	Fee	422	adj Est Lee W Harris & others	N 5 miles	7.94	400.00	3350.63
"	"	"	50	" Foster & McAlexander & others	" "	2.00		100.00
Est Andrew Wright	Nelson	Fee	352	adj Est Lee W Harris & others	N 6 miles	7.00	400.00	2494.00
Jesse Wright	Nelson	Fee	130	adj Benjn Camden & others	W 15 miles	8.88	300.00	1145.30
Geo G, Shelton, Wm & Danl L Wright	Nelson	Fee	285	On Piny River	SW 23 miles	.50		142.50
John B. Wright	Nelson	Fee	1	Adj Thomas Doswell & others	W 24 miles	1.50		1.50
William R. Wright	Nelson	Fee	118	adj William Horsely & others	S 18 miles	3.00		364.00

Appendix: Nelson County, Virginia, 1845 Land Tax List:

District of John H Wingfield:

Name of Owner [continued from prior page]	Am't of Tax on the whole tract at the legal rate	Explanation of alterations during the preceding year especially from whom transferred	Identification
Est James Wright	3.36		Estate of 1839 James Wright of Nelson County, son of William Wright (Amherst County)
"	.10		
Est Andrew Wright	2.50		Estate of 1816 Andrew Wright of Nelson County, son of William Wright (Amherst County)
Jesse Wright	1.15		1850 Jesse Wright of Nelson County, son of 1799 Benjamin Wright of Amherst County and grandson of 1767 Francis Wright of Amherst County
Geo G, Shelton, Wm & Danl L Wright	.15		George G. Wright, son of 1850 Jesse Wright of Nelson County, grandson of 1799 Benjamin Wright of Amherst County, and great grandson of 1767 Francis Wright of Amherst County and 1874 Shelton Wright of Nelson County, son of 1850 Jesse Wright of Nelson County, grandson of 1799 Benjamin Wright of Amherst County, and great grandson of 1767 Francis Wright of Amherst County and 1870 William Wright of Amherst County, son of 1850 Jesse Wright of Nelson County, grandson of 1799 Benjamin Wright of Amherst County, and great grandson of 1767 Francis Wright of Amherst County and 1882 Daniel L. Wright of Amherst County, son of 1850 Jesse Wright of Nelson County, grandson of 1799 Benjamin Wright of Amherst County, and great grandson of 1767 Francis Wright of Amherst County
John B. Wright	.01		John B. Wright, son of 1861 Benjamin Wright of Nelson County, grandson of 1816 Andrew Wright of Nelson County, and great grandson of William Wright (Amherst County)
William R. Wright	.36		1871 William R. Wright of Buckingham County, son of 1842 Thomas Wright of Buckingham County

Appendix: Nelson County, Virginia, 1845 Land Tax List:

District of John H Wingfield:

Name of Owner	Residence	Estate whether held in fee simple for life &c	No. of Acres	Description of the land, as to watercourses, mountains and contiguous tracts	Distance and bearing from the court house	Value of land per acre, including buildings	Sum added to the land on account of buildings	Total value of the land and buildings
George G Wright	Unknown	Fee	6½	On Piney River	W 16 miles	6.50		42.00
Shelton Wright	Nelson	Fee	230	adj Saml McD. Read & others	SW 15 miles	5.69	500.00	1308.70
Charles Wright	Nelson	Fee	68	On Piny River	W 21 miles	1.00		68.00

Appendix: Nelson County, Virginia, 1845 Land Tax List:

District of John H Wingfield:

Name of Owner [continued from prior page]	Am't of Tax on the whole tract at the legal rate	Explanation of alterations during the preceding year especially from whom transferred	Identification
George G Wright	.05		George G. Wright, son of 1850 Jesse Wright of Nelson County, grandson of 1799 Benjamin Wright of Amherst County, and great grandson of 1767 Francis Wright of Amherst County
Shelton Wright	1.31		1874 Shelton Wright of Nelson County, son of 1850 Jesse Wright of Nelson County, grandson of 1799 Benjamin Wright of Amherst County, and great grandson of 1767 Francis Wright of Amherst County
Charles Wright	.07	From Washington Campbell	Charles Wright, son of Benjamin Wright, grandson of 1830 Moses Wright of Amherst County, great grandson of 1799 Benjamin Wright of Amherst County, and great great grandson of 1767 Francis Wright of Amherst County

1846 LAND TAX LIST

NELSON COUNTY, VIRGINIA

Appendix: Nelson County, Virginia, 1846 Land Tax List:

District of John H Wingfield:

Name of Owner	Residence	Estate whether held in fee simple for life &c	No. of Acres	Description of the land, as to watercourses, mountains and contiguous tracts	Distance and bearing from the court house	Value of land per acre, including buildings	Sum added to the land on account of buildings	Total value of the land and buildings
Est James Wright	Nelson	Fee	422	adj Est Lee W Harris &c	N 5 M	7.90	400.00	3350.63
"	"	"	50	" Jo & D R McAlexr "	" "	2.00		100.00
Est Andrew Wright	Nelson	Fee	352	adj Est Lee W Harris &c	N 5 M	7.10	400.00	2494.00
Jesse Wright	Nelson	Fee	130	adj Benjamin Camden &c	W 15 M	8.88	300.00	1154.40
George G, Shelton, Wm & Danl L Wright	Nelson	Fee	285	On Piney River	SW 23 M	.50		142.50
John B. Wright	Nelson	Fee	1	Adj Thos Doswell &c	W 24 M	1.50		1.50
William R Wright	Nelson	Fee	118	Adj Wm Horsely &c	S 18 M	3.00		364.00

Appendix: Nelson County, Virginia, 1846 Land Tax List:

District of John H Wingfield:

Name of Owner [continued from prior page]	Am't of Tax on the whole tract at the legal rate	Explanation of alterations during the preceding year especially from whom transferred	Identification
Est James Wright	3.36		Estate of 1839 James Wright of Nelson County, son of William Wright (Amherst County)
"	.10		
Est Andrew Wright	2.50		Estate of 1816 Andrew Wright of Nelson County, son of William Wright (Amherst County)
Jesse Wright	1.16		1850 Jesse Wright of Nelson County, son of 1799 Benjamin Wright of Amherst County and grandson of 1767 Francis Wright of Amherst County
George G, Shelton, Wm & Danl L Wright	.15		George G. Wright, son of 1850 Jesse Wright of Nelson County, grandson of 1799 Benjamin Wright of Amherst County, and great grandson of 1767 Francis Wright of Amherst County and 1874 Shelton Wright of Nelson County, son of 1850 Jesse Wright of Nelson County, grandson of 1799 Benjamin Wright of Amherst County, and great grandson of 1767 Francis Wright of Amherst County and 1870 William Wright of Amherst County, son of 1850 Jesse Wright of Nelson County, grandson of 1799 Benjamin Wright of Amherst County, and great grandson of 1767 Francis Wright of Amherst County and 1882 Daniel L. Wright of Amherst County, son of 1850 Jesse Wright of Nelson County, grandson of 1799 Benjamin Wright of Amherst County, and great grandson of 1767 Francis Wright of Amherst County
John B. Wright	.01		John B. Wright, son of 1861 Benjamin Wright of Nelson County, grandson of 1816 Andrew Wright of Nelson County, and great grandson of William Wright (Amherst County)
William R. Wright	.36		1871 William R. Wright of Buckingham County, son of 1842 Thomas Wright of Buckingham County

Appendix: Nelson County, Virginia, 1846 Land Tax List:

District of John H Wingfield:

Name of Owner	Residence	Estate whether held in fee simple for life &c	No. of Acres	Description of the land, as to watercourses, mountains and contiguous tracts	Distance and bearing from the court house	Value of land per acre, including buildings	Sum added to the land on account of buildings	Total value of the land and buildings
Geo G Wright	Unknown	Fee	6½	On Piney River	W 16 M	6.50		42.00
Charles Wright	Nelson	Fee	68	On Piney River	W 20 M	1.00		68.00
Nelson Wright	Nelson	Fee	88-7/8	lot No 8 Est Jacob Pucket	N 8 M	2.90		257.74

Appendix: Nelson County, Virginia, 1846 Land Tax List:

District of John H Wingfield:

Name of Owner [continued from prior page]	Am't of Tax on the whole tract at the legal rate	Explanation of alterations during the preceding year especially from whom transferred	Identification
Geo G Wright	.05		George G. Wright, son of 1850 Jesse Wright of Nelson County, grandson of 1799 Benjamin Wright of Amherst County, and great grandson of 1767 Francis Wright of Amherst County
Charles Wright	.07		Charles Wright, son of Benjamin Wright, grandson of 1830 Moses Wright of Amherst County, great grandson of 1799 Benjamin Wright of Amherst County, and great great grandson of 1767 Francis Wright of Amherst County
Nelson Wright	.26	from Est Jacob Pucket	Nelson Wright, son of ____ Wright, grandson of 1839 James Wright of Nelson County, and great grandson of William Wright (Amherst County)

1847 LAND TAX LIST

NELSON COUNTY, VIRGINIA

Appendix: Nelson County, Virginia, 1847 Land Tax List:

District of John H Wingfield:

Name of Owner	Residence	Estate whether held in fee simple for life &c	No. of Acres	Description of the land, as to watercourses, mountains and contiguous tracts	Distance and bearing from the court house	Value of land per acre, including buildings	Sum added to the land on account of buildings	Total value of the land and buildings
Est James Wright	Nelson	Fee	422	Adjoining Est Lee W Harris & others	N 5 Miles	7.90	400.00	3350.68
"	"	"	50	" J R & D K McAlexander	" "	2.00		100.00
Est Andrew Wright	Nelson	Fee	352	Adjoining Est Lee W Harris & others	N 5 Miles	7.10	400.00	2494.00
Jesse Wright	Nelson	Fee	130	Adjoining Benjamin Camden & others	W 15 Miles	8.88	300.00	1154.40
_ Shelton, Wm & D L Wright	Nelson	Fee	285	On Piney River	SW 23 Miles	.50		142.50
John B. Wright	Nelson	Fee	1	Adj Thomas Doswell & others	W 24 Miles	1.50		1.50
George G Wright	Unknown	Fee	6½	On Piney River	W 16 Miles	6.50		42.00

Appendix: Nelson County, Virginia, 1847 Land Tax List:

District of John H Wingfield:

Name of Owner [continued from prior page]	Am't of Tax on the whole tract at the legal rate	Explanation of alterations during the preceding year especially from whom transferred	Identification
Est James Wright	3.36		Estate of 1839 James Wright of Nelson County, son of William Wright (Amherst County)
"	.10		
Est Andrew Wright	2.50		Estate of 1816 Andrew Wright of Nelson County, son of William Wright (Amherst County)
Jesse Wright	1.16		1850 Jesse Wright of Nelson County, son of 1799 Benjamin Wright of Amherst County and grandson of 1767 Francis Wright of Amherst County
_ Shelton, Wm & D L Wright	.15		George G. Wright, son of 1850 Jesse Wright of Nelson County, grandson of 1799 Benjamin Wright of Amherst County, and great grandson of 1767 Francis Wright of Amherst County and 1874 Shelton Wright of Nelson County, son of 1850 Jesse Wright of Nelson County, grandson of 1799 Benjamin Wright of Amherst County, and great grandson of 1767 Francis Wright of Amherst County and 1870 William Wright of Amherst County, son of 1850 Jesse Wright of Nelson County, grandson of 1799 Benjamin Wright of Amherst County, and great grandson of 1767 Francis Wright of Amherst County and 1882 Daniel L. Wright of Amherst County, son of 1850 Jesse Wright of Nelson County, grandson of 1799 Benjamin Wright of Amherst County, and great grandson of 1767 Francis Wright of Amherst County
John B. Wright	.11		John B. Wright, son of 1861 Benjamin Wright of Nelson County, grandson of 1816 Andrew Wright of Nelson County, and great grandson of William Wright (Amherst County)
George G Wright	.05		George G. Wright, son of 1850 Jesse Wright of Nelson County, grandson of 1799 Benjamin Wright of Amherst County, and great grandson of 1767 Francis Wright of Amherst County

Appendix: Nelson County, Virginia, 1847 Land Tax List:

District of John H Wingfield:

Name of Owner	Residence	Estate whether held in fee simple for life &c	No. of Acres	Description of the land, as to watercourses, mountains and contiguous tracts	Distance and bearing from the court house	Value of land per acre, including buildings	Sum added to the land on account of buildings	Total value of the land and buildings
Charles Wright	Nelson	Fee	68	On Piny River	W 20 Miles	1.00		68.00
Nelson Wright	Nelson	Fee	88-7/8	Lot No 8 from Est Jacob Pucket	N 8 Miles	2.90		257.74

Appendix: Nelson County, Virginia, 1847 Land Tax List:

District of John H Wingfield:

Name of Owner [continued from prior page]	Am't of Tax on the whole tract at the legal rate	Explanation of alterations during the preceding year especially from whom transferred	Identification
Charles Wright	.07		Charles Wright, son of Benjamin Wright, grandson of 1830 Moses Wright of Amherst County, great grandson of 1799 Benjamin Wright of Amherst County, and great great grandson of 1767 Francis Wright of Amherst County
Nelson Wright	.26		Nelson Wright, son of ____ Wright, grandson of 1839 James Wright of Nelson County, and great grandson of William Wright (Amherst County)

1848 LAND TAX LIST

NELSON COUNTY, VIRGINIA

Appendix: Nelson County, Virginia, 1848 Land Tax List:

District of John H Wingfield:

Name of Owner	Residence	Estate whether held in fee simple for life &c	No. of Acres	Description of the land, as to watercourses, mountains and contiguous tracts	Distance and bearing from the court house	Value of land per acre, including buildings	Sum added to the land on account of buildings	Total value of the land and buildings
Est James Wright	Nelson	Fee	422	Adj Est Lee W Harris & others	N 5 Miles	7.90	400.00	3350.68
"	"	"	50	" J R & D K McAlexander & others	" "	2.00		100.00
Est Andrew Wright	Nelson	Fee	352	Adj Est Lee W Harris & others	N 5 Miles	7.10	400.00	2494.00
Jesse Wright	Nelson	Fee	130	Adj Benjamin Camden & others	W 15 Miles	8.88	300.00	1154.40
Geo G, Shelton, Wm & D L Wright	Nelson	Fee	285	On Piney River	SW 23 Miles	.50		142.50
John B. Wright	Nelson	Fee	1	Adj Thomas Doswell & others	W 24 Miles	1.50		1.50

Appendix: Nelson County, Virginia, 1848 Land Tax List:

District of John H Wingfield:

Name of Owner [continued from prior page]	Am't of Tax on the whole tract at the legal rate	Explanation of alterations during the preceding year especially from whom transferred	Identification
Est James Wright	3.36		Estate of 1839 James Wright of Nelson County, son of William Wright (Amherst County)
"	.10		
Est Andrew Wright	2.50		Estate of 1816 Andrew Wright of Nelson County, son of William Wright (Amherst County)
Jesse Wright	1.16		1850 Jesse Wright of Nelson County, son of 1799 Benjamin Wright of Amherst County and grandson of 1767 Francis Wright of Amherst County
Geo G, Shelton, Wm & D L Wright	.15		George G. Wright, son of 1850 Jesse Wright of Nelson County, grandson of 1799 Benjamin Wright of Amherst County, and great grandson of 1767 Francis Wright of Amherst County and 1874 Shelton Wright of Nelson County, son of 1850 Jesse Wright of Nelson County, grandson of 1799 Benjamin Wright of Amherst County, and great grandson of 1767 Francis Wright of Amherst County and 1870 William Wright of Amherst County, son of 1850 Jesse Wright of Nelson County, grandson of 1799 Benjamin Wright of Amherst County, and great grandson of 1767 Francis Wright of Amherst County and 1882 Daniel L. Wright of Amherst County, son of 1850 Jesse Wright of Nelson County, grandson of 1799 Benjamin Wright of Amherst County, and great grandson of 1767 Francis Wright of Amherst County
John B. Wright	.11		John B. Wright, son of 1861 Benjamin Wright of Nelson County, grandson of 1816 Andrew Wright of Nelson County, and great grandson of William Wright (Amherst County)

1394(051607)

Appendix: Nelson County, Virginia, 1848 Land Tax List:

District of John H Wingfield:

Name of Owner	Residence	Estate whether held in fee simple for life &c	No. of Acres	Description of the land, as to watercourses, mountains and contiguous tracts	Distance and bearing from the court house	Value of land per acre, including buildings	Sum added to the land on account of buildings	Total value of the land and buildings
George G Wright	Unknown	Fee	6½	On Piny River	W 16 Miles	6.50		42.00
Charles Wright	Amherst	Fee	68	On Piny River	W 20 Miles	1.00		68.00
Nelson Wright	Amherst	Fee	88-7/8	Adj Wm H Pucket & others	N 9 Miles	2.90		257.74

Appendix: Nelson County, Virginia, 1848 Land Tax List:

District of John H Wingfield:

Name of Owner [continued from prior page]	Am't of Tax on the whole tract at the legal rate	Explanation of alterations during the preceding year especially from whom transferred	Identification
George G Wright	.05		George G. Wright, son of 1850 Jesse Wright of Nelson County, grandson of 1799 Benjamin Wright of Amherst County, and great grandson of 1767 Francis Wright of Amherst County
Charles Wright	.07		Charles Wright, son of Benjamin Wright, grandson of 1830 Moses Wright of Amherst County, great grandson of 1799 Benjamin Wright of Amherst County, and great great grandson of 1767 Francis Wright of Amherst County
Nelson Wright	.26		Nelson Wright, son of ____ Wright, grandson of 1839 James Wright of Nelson County, and great grandson of William Wright (Amherst County)

1849 LAND TAX LIST

NELSON COUNTY, VIRGINIA

Appendix: Nelson County, Virginia, 1849 Land Tax List:

District of John H Wingfield:

Name of Owner	Residence	Estate whether held in fee simple for life &c	No. of Acres	Description of the land, as to watercourses, mountains and contiguous tracts	Distance and bearing from the court house	Value of land per acre, including buildings	Sum added to the land on account of buildings	Total value of the land and buildings
Est James Wright	Nelson	Fee	422	Adj Est Lee W Harris & others	N 5 Miles	7.90	400.00	3350.68
"	"	"	50	"J R & D K McAlexander & others	" " "	2.00		100.00
Est Andrew Wright	Nelson	Fee	352	Adj Est Lee W Harris & others	N 5 Miles	7.10	400.00	2494.00
Jesse Wright	Nelson	Fee	130	Adj Benjamin Camden & others	W 16 Miles	8.88	300.00	1154.40
Geo G, Shelton, Wm & Daniel L Wright	Nelson	Fee	285	On Piny River	W 23 Miles	.50		142.50
John B. Wright	Nelson	Fee	1	Adj Thomas Doswell & others	W 24 Miles	1.50		1.50

Appendix: Nelson County, Virginia, 1849 Land Tax List:

District of John H Wingfield:

Name of Owner [continued from prior page]	Am't of Tax on the whole tract at the legal rate	Explanation of alterations during the preceding year especially from whom transferred	Identification
Est James Wright	3.36		Estate of 1839 James Wright of Nelson County, son of William Wright (Amherst County)
"	.10		
Est Andrew Wright	2.50		Estate of 1816 Andrew Wright of Nelson County, son of William Wright (Amherst County)
Jesse Wright	1.16		1850 Jesse Wright of Nelson County, son of 1799 Benjamin Wright of Amherst County and grandson of 1767 Francis Wright of Amherst County
Geo G, Shelton, Wm & Daniel L Wright	.15		George G. Wright, son of 1850 Jesse Wright of Nelson County, grandson of 1799 Benjamin Wright of Amherst County, and great grandson of 1767 Francis Wright of Amherst County and 1874 Shelton Wright of Nelson County, son of 1850 Jesse Wright of Nelson County, grandson of 1799 Benjamin Wright of Amherst County, and great grandson of 1767 Francis Wright of Amherst County and 1870 William Wright of Amherst County, son of 1850 Jesse Wright of Nelson County, grandson of 1799 Benjamin Wright of Amherst County, and great grandson of 1767 Francis Wright of Amherst County and 1882 Daniel L. Wright of Amherst County, son of 1850 Jesse Wright of Nelson County, grandson of 1799 Benjamin Wright of Amherst County, and great grandson of 1767 Francis Wright of Amherst County
John B. Wright	.11		John B. Wright, son of 1861 Benjamin Wright of Nelson County, grandson of 1816 Andrew Wright of Nelson County, and great grandson of William Wright (Amherst County)

Appendix: Nelson County, Virginia, 1849 Land Tax List:

District of John H Wingfield:

Name of Owner	Residence	Estate whether held in fee simple for life &c	No. of Acres	Description of the land, as to watercourses, mountains and contiguous tracts	Distance and bearing from the court house	Value of land per acre, including buildings	Sum added to the land on account of buildings	Total value of the land and buildings
George G Wright	Unknown	Fee	6½	On Piny River	W 16 Miles	6.50		42.25
Charles Wright	Nelson	Fee	68	On Piny River	W 20 Miles	1.00		68.00
Nelson Wright	Nelson	Fee	88-7/8	Adj Wm H Pucket & others	N 8 Miles	2.90		257.74
Robert Wright	Nelson	Fee	37-2/3	Adj James Lobban & others	NW 18 Miles	5.00		188.33

Appendix: Nelson County, Virginia, 1849 Land Tax List:

District of John H Wingfield:

Name of Owner [continued from prior page]	Am't of Tax on the whole tract at the legal rate	Explanation of alterations during the preceding year especially from whom transferred	Identification
George G Wright	.05		George G. Wright, son of 1850 Jesse Wright of Nelson County, grandson of 1799 Benjamin Wright of Amherst County, and great grandson of 1767 Francis Wright of Amherst County
Charles Wright	.07		Charles Wright, son of Benjamin Wright, grandson of 1830 Moses Wright of Amherst County, great grandson of 1799 Benjamin Wright of Amherst County, and great great grandson of 1767 Francis Wright of Amherst County
Nelson Wright	.26		Nelson Wright, son of ____ Wright, grandson of 1839 James Wright of Nelson County, and great grandson of William Wright (Amherst County)
Robert Wright	.19	from John Lobban	

1850 LAND TAX LIST

NELSON COUNTY, VIRGINIA

Appendix: Nelson County, Virginia, 1850 Land Tax List:

District of John H Wingfield:

Name of Owner	Residence	Estate whether held in fee simple for life &c	No. of Acres	Description of the land, as to watercourses, mountains and contiguous tracts	Distance and earing from the court house	Value of land per acre, including buildings	Sum added to the land on account of buildings	Total value of the land and buildings
Mary Wright	Nelson	Fee	422	Adj Est L W Harris & others	N 5 Miles	7.90	400.00	3350.68
"	"	"	50	" J R & D R McAlexander & others	" "	2.00		100.00
Est Andrew Wright	Nelson	Fee	352	Adj Est L W Harris & others	N 5 Miles	7.10	400.00	2494.00
Jesse Wright	Nelson	Fee	130	Adj Benja Camden & others	W 15 Miles	8.88	300.00	1154.40
_ G Shelton, Wm & D L Wright	Nelson	Fee	285	On Piny River	W 23 Miles	.50		142.50
John B. Wright	Nelson	Fee	1	Adj Thos Doswell & others	W 24 Miles	1.50		1.50

Appendix: Nelson County, Virginia, 1850 Land Tax List:

District of John H Wingfield:

Name of Owner [continued from prior page]	Am't of Tax on the whole tract at the legal rate	Explanation of alterations during the preceding year especially from whom transferred	Identification
Mary Wright	3.36	From Est James Wright	Mary "Polly" Wright, daughter of 1839 James Wright of Nelson County and grandson of William Wright (Amherst County)
"	.10	" " " "	
Est Andrew Wright	2.50		Estate of 1816 Andrew Wright of Nelson County, son of William Wright (Amherst County)
Jesse Wright	1.16		1850 Jesse Wright of Nelson County, son of 1799 Benjamin Wright of Amherst County and grandson of 1767 Francis Wright of Amherst County
_ G Shelton, Wm & D L Wright	.15		George G. Wright, son of 1850 Jesse Wright of Nelson County, grandson of 1799 Benjamin Wright of Amherst County, and great grandson of 1767 Francis Wright of Amherst County and
1874 Shelton Wright of Nelson County, son of 1850 Jesse Wright of Nelson County, grandson of 1799 Benjamin Wright of Amherst County, and great grandson of 1767 Francis Wright of Amherst County and
1870 William Wright of Amherst County, son of 1850 Jesse Wright of Nelson County, grandson of 1799 Benjamin Wright of Amherst County, and great grandson of 1767 Francis Wright of Amherst County and
1882 Daniel L. Wright of Amherst County, son of 1850 Jesse Wright of Nelson County, grandson of 1799 Benjamin Wright of Amherst County, and great grandson of 1767 Francis Wright of Amherst County
John B. Wright	.01		John B. Wright, son of 1861 Benjamin Wright of Nelson County, grandson of 1816 Andrew Wright of Nelson County, and great grandson of William Wright (Amherst County)

Appendix: Nelson County, Virginia, 1850 Land Tax List:

District of John H Wingfield:

Name of Owner	Residence	Estate whether held in fee simple for life &c	No. of Acres	Description of the land, as to watercourses, mountains and contiguous tracts	Distance and earing from the court house	Value of land per acre, including buildings	Sum added to the land on account of buildings	Total value of the land and buildings
George G Wright	Nelson	Fee	6½	On Piney River	W 15 Miles	6.50		42.25
Charles Wright	Nelson	Fee	68	On Piney River	W 20 Miles	1.00		68.00
Nelson Wright	Nelson	Fee	88-7/8	Adj Wm H Pucket & others	N 8 Miles	2.90		257.74
Robert Wright	Nelson	Fee	37-2/3	Adj James Lobban & others	NW 18 Miles	5.00		188.33
"	"	"	75	" " " "	" " "	5.00		375.50

Appendix: Nelson County, Virginia, 1850 Land Tax List:

District of John H Wingfield:

Name of Owner [continued from prior page]	Am't of Tax on the whole tract at the legal rate	Explanation of alterations during the preceding year especially from whom transferred	Identification
George G Wright	.05		George G. Wright, son of 1850 Jesse Wright of Nelson County, grandson of 1799 Benjamin Wright of Amherst County, and great grandson of 1767 Francis Wright of Amherst County
Charles Wright	.07		Charles Wright, son of Benjamin Wright, grandson of 1830 Moses Wright of Amherst County, great grandson of 1799 Benjamin Wright of Amherst County, and great great grandson of 1767 Francis Wright of Amherst County
Nelson Wright	.26		Nelson Wright, son of ____ Wright, grandson of 1839 James Wright of Nelson County, and great grandson of William Wright (Amherst County)
Robert Wright	.19		
	.38		

INDEX

Boswell, Thomas, 103, 109, 115
Bryant, P., 24, 30
Bryant, Parmenas, 18
Cabell, Frederick, 101
Camden, Benja, 199
Camden, Benjamin, 145, 157, 163, 174, 181, 187, 193
Camden, Benjn, 139, 151, 169
Camden, J., 28
Camden, Jno, 10, 16, 22
Camden, John, 8, 34, 40, 46, 50, 54, 58, 62, 66, 70, 74, 78, 82, 86, 90, 94, 98, 103, 109, 115, 121, 127, 133
Clarke, Nathl, 104
Doswell, Thomas, 121, 133, 139, 145, 151, 157, 163, 169, 181, 187, 193, 199
Edmond, Saml, 8, 62
Edmonds, Samuel, 46, 50, 54, 58, 66
Edmunds, S, 18, 22, 30, 42
Edmunds, Saul, 36
Ellis, Geo G., 94, 98, 103, 109
Ellis, George G., 82, 83, 86, 87, 90, 91, 95, 99, 104, 110, 115, 116, 121, 122, 127, 128
Garland, D S, 8, 10, 12
Glass, T, 10, 12
Glass, Thos, 16
Harris, Jno W, 42
Harris, L W, 10, 199
Harris, Lee W, 66, 70, 74, 78, 82, 86, 90, 94, 98, 103, 109, 114, 121, 127, 133, 139, 145, 151, 157, 163, 169, 175, 181 187, 193
Horsely, William, 163, 169
Horsley, Jno, 139
Horsley, John, 100, 105, 111, 123, 129, 133, 145
Hubbard, Robert T, 127
Hutton, E W, 109, 115

Hutton, R Y, 121
Hutton, Robt, 109, 115
Hutton, W H, 12
Irving, Charles, 55
Jones, George, 124
Lilliput(?), W, 19
Lobban, James, 195, 201
Lobban, John, 196
Loftus, N., 16
Loving, J, 22, 28
Martin, Peter, 23
McAlexander, Alexander, 70, 71, 74, 78, 82, 86
McAlexander, Alexr, 90, 94, 98, 103, 109, 115, 127, 133, 139, 145
McAlexander, D K, 181, 187, 193
McAlexander, D R, 199
McAlexander, Foster S, 151, 157, 163
McAlexander, J R, 181, 187, 193, 199
McAlexander, John, 47
McAlexr, Alexr, 121
McAlexr, D R, 175
McAlexr, Jo, 175
Melton, Jno, 10, 22
Melton, John, 16, 46
Meltons, J, 28
Milton, John, 12
Murray, John W, 54, 62
Murray, W, 58
Pucket, Jacob, 177, 178, 183
Pucket, Wm H, 189, 195, 201
Read, Saml McD, 141, 147, 153, 159, 165, 171
Reese, Saml McD, 123
Reid, Saml McD, 129, 135
Shelton, Geo G, 151, 152
Shelton, George G, 157, 158, 163, 164, 133, 134
Shelton, H., 34

Shelton, J, 12
Shelton, Jno, 34
Shelton, Jos, 10, 40
Shelton, Joseph, 16
Shelton, W H, 16, 22, 28
Shelton, William H, 46, 50, 58, 62
Shelton, Wm H, 40
Wright, A, 10, 12, 16, 22, 28
Wright, Andrew, 2, 4, 6, 8, 10, 12, 13, 16, 17, 22, 23, 28, 29, 34, 35, 40, 41, 46, 47, 50, 51, 54, 58, 59, 62, 63, 66, 67, 70, 71, 74, 75, 78, 79, 82, 83, 86, 87, 90, 91, 94, 95, 98, 99, 103, 104, 109, 110, 115, 116, 121, 122, 127, 128, 133, 134, 139, 140, 145, 146, 151, 152, 157, 158, 163, 164, 169, 170, 175, 176, 181, 182, 187, 188, 193, 194, 199, 200
Wright, Archilles, 2, 4
Wright, Austin, 54, 55, 58, 59, 62, 63, 66, 67, 70, 71, 74, 75, 78, 79, 82, 83, 86, 87, 90, 91, 94, 95, 98, 99, 103, 104, 109, 110, 115, 116, 121, 122, 127, 128
Wright, Benjamin, 30, 31, 42, 43
Wright, Benjn, 30, 31
Wright, Charles, 171, 172, 177, 178, 183, 184, 189, 190, 195, 196, 201, 202
Wright, D. L., 151, 152, 157, 158, 163, 164, 181, 182, 187, 188, 199, 200
Wright, Daniel L, 82, 83, 86, 87, 90, 91, 94, 95, 98, 99, 103, 109, 110, 115, 116, 127, 128, 133, 134, 145, 146, 193, 194
Wright, Danl L, 104, 121, 122, 139, 140, 169, 170, 175, 176
Wright, Eid(?) William, 145
Wright, Geo G, 147, 148, 169, 170, 177, 178, 187, 188, 193, 194

Wright, George G, 117, 118, 123, 124, 129, 130, 135, 136, 141, 142, 151, 152, 159, 160, 163, 164, 171, 172, 175, 176, 181, 182, 189, 190, 195, 196, 201, 202

Wright, James, 2, 4, 6, 8, 12, 13, 16, 17, 22, 23, 28, 29, 34, 35, 40, 41, 46, 47, 50, 51, 54, 55, 58, 59, 62, 63, 66, 67, 70, 71, 74, 75, 78, 79, 82, 83, 86, 87, 90, 91, 94, 95, 98, 99, 103, 104, 109, 110, 115, 116, 121, 122, 127, 128, 133, 134, 139, 140, 145, 146, 151, 152, 157, 158, 163, 164, 169, 170, 175, 176, 181, 182, 187, 188, 192, 194, 200

Wright, Jas., 10

Wright, Jesse, 2, 4, 6, 8, 10, 12, 13, 16, 17, 22, 23, 28, 29, 34, 35, 40, 41, 46, 47, 50, 51, 54, 55, 58, 59, 62, 63, 66, 67, 70, 71, 74, 75, 78, 79, 82, 83, 86, 87, 90, 91, 94, 95, 98, 99, 103, 104, 109, 110, 115, 116, 121, 122, 127, 128, 133, 134, 139, 140, 145, 146, 151, 152, 157, 158, 163, 164, 169, 170, 175, 176, 181, 182, 187, 188, 193, 194, 199, 200

Wright, Jno, 28, 29, 34, 35

Wright, John, 2, 4, 6, 8, 12, 13, 40, 41, 46, 47, 55

Wright, John B., 86, 87, 90, 91, 94, 95, 98, 99, 103, 104, 109, 110, 115, 116, 121, 122, 127, 128, 133, 134, 139, 140, 145, 146, 151, 152, 157, 158, 163, 164, 169, 170, 175, 176, 181, 182, 187, 188, 193, 194, 199, 200

Wright, Jordan, 2, 4, 6, 8, 10, 12, 13, 18, 19, 22, 23, 30, 31, 36, 37, 42, 43, 46, 47, 50, 51, 54, 55, 58, 59, 62, 63, 66, 67

Wright, Mary, 199, 200

Wright, Moses, 2, 4, 6, 8, 10, 12, 13, 16, 17, 22, 23, 28, 29, 34, 35, 40, 41

Wright, Nelson, 177, 178, 183, 184, 189, 190, 195, 196, 201, 202

Wright, Ro, 10, 12, 13 29

Wright, Robert, 6, 8, 16, 17, 22, 23, 195, 196, 201, 202

Wright, Robt, 2, 4

Wright, Shelton, 82, 83, 86, 87, 90, 91, 94, 95, 98, 99, 103, 104, 109, 110, 115, 116, 121, 122, 123, 124, 127, 128, 129, 130, 135, 136, 141, 142, 145, 146, 147, 148, 153, 154, 159, 160, 165, 166, 169, 170, 171, 172, 175, 176, 181, 182, 187, 188, 193, 194, 199, 200

Wright, Thomas, 100, 101, 105, 106, 111, 112, 117, 118, 123, 124, 129, 130, 133, 134, 139, 140, 145, 146, 152, 158

Wright, W, 34, 22

Wright, William, 8, 30, 31, 34, 35, 40, 41, 46, 47, 50, 51, 54, 55, 58, 59, 62, 63, 66, 67, 70, 71, 74, 75, 78, 79, 82, 83, 86, 87, 90, 91, 94, 95, 98, 99, 103, 104, 115, 116, 127, 128, 133, 134

Wright, William R, 151, 157, 163, 175, 152, 158, 164, 169, 170, 176

Wright, Wm, 2, 4, 6, 10, 12, 13, 16, 17, 18, 19, 22, 23, 24, 25, 28, 29, 62, 90, 94, 98, 103, 109, 110, 115, 121, 122, 127, 139, 140, 145, 146, 151, 152, 157, 158, 163, 164, 169, 170, 175, 176, 181, 182, 187, 188, 193, 194, 199, 200

Wright (BS), John, 4, 6, 8, 10, 28, 29, 34, 35, 50, 51, 54, 58, 59, 62, 63

Wright (SR), Jno, 16, 17

Wright (SR), John, 10

Wright BS, Jno, 22, 23

Wright BS, John, 12, 13, 16, 17

Other Heritage Books by Robert N. Grant

Identifying the Wrights in the Goochland County, Virginia Tithe Lists, 1732-84

The Identification of 1809 William Wright of Franklin County, Virginia, as the Son of 1792 John Wright of Fauquier County, Virginia, and Elizabeth (Bronaugh) (Darnall) Wright

Wright Family Birth Records (1853-1896) and Marriage Records (1788-1915): Franklin County, Virginia, 1853-1896

Wright Family Birth Records, 1853-1896; Marriage Records, 1761-1900; Census Records, 1810-1900, in Amherst County, Virginia

Wright Family Birth Records, 1853-1896; Marriage Records, 1808-1910; Census Records, 1810-1900; Patent Deeds and Land Grants; Deed Records, 1808-1910; Death Records, 1853-1896; Probate Records, 1808-1900, in Nelson County, Virginia

Wright Family Birth Records (1853-1896) and Marriage Records (1782-1900): Campbell County, Virginia

Wright Family Birth Records, Marriage Records, and Personal Property Tax Lists: Appomattox County, Virginia

Wright Family Census Records, Deed Records, Land Tax Lists, Death Records and Probate Records: Appomattox County, Virginia

Wright Family Census Records: Bedford County, Virginia, 1810-1900

Wright Family Census Records: Campbell County, Virginia, 1810-1900

Wright Family Census Records: Franklin County, Virginia, 1810-1900

Wright Family Death Records (1853-1920), Cemetery Records by Cemetery, and Probate Records (1782-1900): Campbell County, Virginia

Wright Family Death Records (1854-1920), Cemetery Records by Cemetery, and Probate Records (1785-1928): Franklin County, Virginia

Wright Family Death, Cemetery and Probate Records: Bedford County, Virginia

Wright Family Deed Records (1782-1900) and Land Tax List (1782-1850): Campbell County, Virginia

Wright Family Land Grants (1785-1900) and Deed Records (1785-1897): Franklin County, Virginia

Wright Family Land Grants, Deed Records, Land Tax List, Death Records, Probate Records: Prince Edward County, Virginia

Wright Family Land Records: Bedford County, Virginia

Wright Family Land Tax Lists: Franklin County, Virginia, 1786-1860

Wright Family Land Tax Records: Amherst County, Virginia, 1782-1850

Wright Family Land Tax Records: Nelson County, Virginia, 1809-1850

Wright Family Patent Deeds and Land Grants, 1761-1900, Deed Records, 1761-1903; Chancery Court Files, 1804-1900; Death Records, 1853-1920; Cemetery Records by Cemetery; and Probate Records, 1761-1900, in Amherst County, Virginia

Wright Family Personal Property Tax Lists: Amherst County, Virginia, 1782-1850

Wright Family Personal Property Tax Lists: Campbell County, Virginia, 1785-1850

Wright Family Personal Property Tax Lists: Franklin County, Virginia, 1786-1850

Wright Family Personal Property Tax Lists: Nelson County, Virginia, 1809-1850

Wright Family Personal Property Tax Records for Bedford County, Virginia, 1782 to 1850

Wright Family Records: Births in Bedford County, Virginia

Wright Family Records: Land Tax List, Bedford County, Virginia, 1782-1850

Wright Family Records: Lynchburg, Virginia Birth Records (1853-1896), Marriage Records (1805-1900), Marriage Notices (1794-1880), Census Records (1900), Deed Records (1805-1900), Death Records (1853-1896), Probate Records (1805-1900)

Wright Family Records: Marriages in Bedford County, Virginia

Wright Family Records: Prince Edward County, Virginia Birth Records, Marriage Records, Election Polls, and Tithe List, Personal Property Tax List, Census